Next-Gen Mainframe: Mastering Modern Automation Techniques

Mainframes

Isaac Nangan

Published by Isaac Nangan, 2024.

NEXT-GEN MAINFRAME: MASTERING MODERN AUTOMATION TECHNIQUES

First edition. January 31, 2024.

ISBN: 978-9815194432

Written by Isaac Nangan.

Table of Contents

To Coleen, Sky and Neo. You are my inspirations.

Next-Gen Mainframe: Mastering Modern Automation Techniques

Isaac Nangan

Preface

In the ever-evolving landscape of technology, the longevity and resilience of mainframe computers stand as a testament to their unparalleled reliability and efficiency. However, as the digital era marches forward, these robust machines face new challenges and opportunities. "Next-Gen Mainframe: Mastering Modern Automation Techniques" is a journey into the heart of modernizing these computing giants through the lens of automation.

This book is born from a dual realization: the undiminished relevance of mainframes in critical sectors and the transformative power of modern automation technologies. It's crafted for IT professionals, mainframe administrators, and technology enthusiasts looking to bridge the gap between traditional mainframe operations and cutting-edge automation strategies.

As you delve into these pages, you'll embark on a comprehensive exploration. From the historic evolution of mainframes to the intricate workings of their architecture, we lay a foundation upon which the principles of automation are built. We dissect modern tools and technologies, providing insights into how artificial intelligence, machine learning, and cloud computing are revolutionizing mainframe operations. The chapters are peppered with real-world case studies, offering a glimpse into successful automation strategies and the lessons learned from them.

This book doesn't just aim to inform; it strives to equip you with practical knowledge and an understanding of emerging trends to prepare you for the future of mainframe computing. Whether you're seeking to enhance your professional skills or satisfy a curiosity about the intersection of mainframes and modern automation, this book offers a comprehensive guide to understanding and implementing these technologies.

As we stand at the cusp of a new era in computing, "Next-Gen Mainframe: Mastering Modern Automation Techniques" invites you to be part of the exciting journey of transforming mainframes into dynamic, automated powerhouses of the digital age.

Prologue

In a world dominated by rapid technological advancements, there lies an unsung hero in the shadows of computing history: the mainframe. These powerful machines, often perceived as relics of a bygone era, continue to pulsate at the heart of global commerce, managing critical operations from financial transactions to airline reservations.

Imagine stepping into a vast data center, the hum of massive machines resonating around you. Here, in these electronically charged corridors, the legacy of decades of computing evolution stands. These mainframes, with their labyrinthine arrays of cables and blinking lights, are not just pieces of technology; they are the custodians of an enduring legacy, silently shouldering the load of massive data processing day in and day out.

But as the digital universe expands and the demands on data processing grow more complex, a question arises: How do these technological titans evolve to meet the needs of the modern era? This is the narrative of transformation, a tale of how automation becomes the key to unlocking a new realm of possibilities for mainframes.

This prologue invites you on an intriguing journey through the annals of computing history, leading up to the present day where innovation meets tradition. We will explore how modern automation techniques breathe new life into these venerable machines, enhancing their efficiency, bolstering security, and ensuring their continued relevance in a world that relentlessly races towards the future.

As we turn the pages, we will witness a metamorphosis. Mainframes, once viewed as static and unchanging, are reimagined through the lens of automation, evolving into agile, efficient, and future-ready systems. This journey is not just about technology; it's a story of adaptation, innovation, and the enduring spirit of human ingenuity.

Welcome to "Next-Gen Mainframe: Mastering Modern Automation Techniques." Prepare to be part of an extraordinary transformation, where the old and the new converge to redefine the future of computing.

Chapter 1. Introduction to Mainframe Automation

1.1. Evolution of Mainframes

Mainframe computers, known for their large size, extensive processing power, and high levels of reliability, have been pivotal in the evolution of computing. This section will trace the journey of mainframes from their inception in the 1950s to their current state. We'll explore how mainframes have continuously adapted to meet changing technology and business needs, focusing on key milestones like the introduction of IBM's System/360 in the 1960s and the shift towards high-capacity, internet-based computing in the 2000s. This historical context sets the stage for understanding why mainframes remain relevant and how they have become prime candidates for modern automation techniques.

1.2. The Need for Automation in the Mainframe Environment

In this section, we'll delve into the reasons driving the need for automation in mainframe environments. Despite their robustness and efficiency, mainframes face challenges like complex legacy systems, a shortage of skilled professionals, and increasing demands for faster processing and real-time data analytics. We'll discuss how automation addresses these challenges, enhancing operational efficiency, reducing human error, and enabling quicker, data-driven decision-making. This part will also highlight how automation in mainframes contributes to cost savings and improved service delivery, making a compelling case for its necessity in today's fast-paced business world.

1.3. Overview of Modern Automation Techniques

This section will provide an overview of modern automation techniques that are reshaping mainframe operations. We'll introduce concepts like robotic process automation (RPA), artificial intelligence (AI), and machine learning (ML), explaining how they apply to mainframe environments. The focus will be on real-world applications, such as AI-driven predictive maintenance, ML-based anomaly detection, and automated batch processing. By showcasing these techniques, this section will illustrate how modern automation not only streamlines operations but also unlocks new capabilities within mainframe systems.

1.1. Evolution of Mainframes

The story of mainframe computers is not just a chronicle of hardware evolution but a reflection of the changing face of technology and business needs over decades. Known for their large size, extensive processing power, and high levels of reliability, mainframes have been pivotal in the evolution of computing, adapting and evolving to remain at the forefront of the technology landscape.

The Inception in the 1950s

Our journey begins in the 1950s, a time when the concept of a computer was synonymous with large, room-sized machines, accessible only to a select few in academia and government. These early mainframes, such as the IBM 701 and UNIVAC, were marvels of their time, capable of processing data at unprecedented speeds. They were primarily used for scientific calculations and governmental purposes, laying the groundwork for more sophisticated computing needs.

Revolution with IBM's System/360 in the 1960s

A significant milestone in mainframe history was the introduction of IBM's System/360 in the 1960s. This family of mainframe computers revolutionized the industry by offering a series of compatible models with varying capacities. For the first time, businesses could upgrade their systems without completely overhauling their existing infrastructure. The System/360 also introduced key features like standardized interfaces and operating systems, which are now foundational concepts in computing.

The Rise of Commercial Computing in the 1970s and 1980s

As we moved into the 1970s and 1980s, mainframes began to dominate commercial computing. They became the backbone of business operations, handling tasks ranging from transaction processing to data management for banks, airlines, and retailers. The era saw enhancements in processing power, storage capabilities, and the introduction of virtualization, which allowed mainframes to run multiple applications and processes simultaneously, further cementing their place in the business world.

Transition to High-Capacity, Internet-Based Computing in the 2000s

The advent of the internet in the late 20th century and its explosive growth in the 2000s brought new challenges and opportunities. Mainframes adapted once more, evolving into high-capacity, internet-based computing systems. This era saw mainframes becoming more integrated with new technologies like web services and cloud computing. They began to support a wider range of applications and operating systems, further broadening their scope and utility.

Present Day and the Role of Mainframes

Today, mainframes continue to be a vital component of the IT infrastructure for many large organizations. They handle massive transaction volumes, manage large databases, and are critical in the fields of finance, healthcare, and government. Despite the rise of distributed computing and cloud services, the reliability, security, and processing power of mainframes make them irreplaceable for certain tasks.

Conclusion: Mainframes as Candidates for Modern Automation

This historical journey underscores why mainframes remain relevant in the modern era. Their ability to adapt and evolve with technological advancements positions them as prime candidates for modern automation techniques. As we delve deeper into the book, we'll explore how the integration of contemporary automation tools and strategies can further enhance the capabilities of these enduring machines, ensuring their relevance in the future of computing.

1.2. The Need for Automation in the Mainframe Environment

While mainframes are renowned for their robustness and efficiency, they are not without challenges in the modern technological landscape. This section delves into the compelling reasons driving the need for automation in mainframe environments, addressing how this evolution is not just beneficial but necessary for these computing behemoths to remain competitive and effective.

Addressing Complex Legacy Systems

Many mainframe systems in operation today are built on legacy technology. These systems, while stable and reliable, often lack the agility and flexibility needed in the rapidly changing digital world. They are built on older code, sometimes several decades old, making them difficult to integrate with newer technologies. Automation introduces modern capabilities into these legacy systems, allowing for more seamless integration with contemporary applications and technologies. It helps bridge the gap between old and new, ensuring that mainframes can continue to serve their critical functions while staying up-to-date with current technological trends.

Combating the Shortage of Skilled Professionals

There's a growing shortage of professionals skilled in mainframe technology, largely due to a generational shift in the workforce. As experienced mainframe professionals retire, there's a notable gap in expertise. Automation can mitigate this challenge by reducing the reliance on specialized knowledge. Automated processes and tools can take over routine, repetitive tasks, freeing up existing staff to focus on more complex issues that require their expertise. This not only addresses the skill gap but also makes mainframe operations more manageable and less dependent on a shrinking talent pool.

Meeting Increasing Demands for Faster Processing and Real-Time Analytics

In an era where speed and data are king, mainframes are increasingly called upon to process vast amounts of data at unprecedented speeds. The demand for real-time analytics and faster processing is not just a matter of efficiency but a competitive necessity in many industries. Automation enables mainframes to meet these demands more effectively. Automated tools can process and analyze data much faster than manual methods, providing real-time insights and significantly speeding up data-intensive operations. This capability is crucial in sectors where timely data processing and analysis can mean the difference between success and failure.

Enhancing Operational Efficiency and Reducing Human Error

Automation in mainframe environments significantly enhances operational efficiency. By automating routine tasks, organizations can optimize their workflows, reduce the time spent on manual processes, and minimize the risk of human error. This increase in efficiency not only speeds up operations but also leads to more consistent and reliable outcomes. As mainframe systems handle critical operations, reducing the margin for error is paramount, and automation plays a key role in achieving this reliability.

Contributing to Cost Savings and Improved Service Delivery

Finally, the integration of automation in mainframe environments can lead to significant cost savings and improved service delivery. Automated systems require less manual intervention, reducing labor costs and allowing human resources to be allocated to more strategic initiatives. Additionally, the increased efficiency and reliability brought about by automation can lead to improved service delivery, enhancing customer satisfaction and strengthening the organization's competitive edge.

Conclusion

The integration of automation into mainframe environments is not just a trend; it's a strategic necessity. By addressing the challenges of legacy systems, skill shortages, increasing data demands, and the need for enhanced efficiency and reduced error, automation paves the way for mainframes to continue playing a crucial role in the digital landscape. It ensures that these powerful machines remain not just operational but optimally functional in today's fast-paced business world.

1.3. Overview of Modern Automation Techniques

The landscape of mainframe automation is continually evolving, with modern techniques reshaping how these systems operate and interact within the broader IT ecosystem. This section provides an overview of these groundbreaking automation technologies, focusing on their applications in mainframe environments and how they are revolutionizing traditional operational models.

Robotic Process Automation (RPA)

Robotic Process Automation (RPA) is a transformative technology that automates repetitive, rule-based tasks that were previously performed manually. In mainframe environments, RPA can be used to automate routine processes like data entry, report generation, and batch job monitoring. This not only speeds up operations but also reduces the risk of human error, leading to more consistent and reliable outcomes. RPA tools can interface with existing mainframe applications, enabling automation without the need for significant changes to the underlying systems.

Artificial Intelligence (AI) and Machine Learning (ML)

AI and ML are at the forefront of modern automation, providing capabilities that go beyond simple task automation. These technologies enable systems to learn from data, identify patterns, and make decisions with minimal human intervention.

- **AI-driven Predictive Maintenance:** In mainframe environments, AI can be used for predictive maintenance, anticipating hardware or software issues before they occur. By analyzing operational data, AI algorithms can identify potential failure points, allowing for proactive maintenance and reducing downtime.
- **ML-based Anomaly Detection:** Machine Learning is particularly effective in anomaly detection, a critical aspect of mainframe operations. ML algorithms can process vast amounts of operational data, identifying outliers and potential security threats that might go unnoticed by human analysts. This capability is crucial for maintaining the integrity and security of mainframe systems, especially in industries dealing with sensitive data.

Automated Batch Processing

Batch processing is a staple of mainframe operations, where large volumes of data are processed at scheduled times. Automation in batch processing can significantly improve efficiency and accuracy. Modern automation tools can schedule and monitor batch jobs, optimize resource allocation, and provide real-time alerts in case of failures or deviations. This not only streamlines the batch processing workflow but also allows for more dynamic scheduling and resource management.

The Integration of Cloud Computing

The integration of cloud computing with mainframe environments is another aspect of modern automation. Cloud-based automation tools can offer scalability, flexibility, and enhanced data analytics capabilities. For mainframes, this means the ability to offload certain tasks to the cloud, such as data storage and analysis, while maintaining core operations on-premise. This hybrid approach allows organizations to leverage the strengths of both mainframes and cloud computing.

Conclusion

Modern automation techniques, including RPA, AI, ML, and cloud integration, are not just streamlining mainframe operations; they are unlocking new capabilities and enabling mainframes to be more adaptable, efficient, and secure in the digital age. By embracing these technologies, organizations can ensure that their mainframe systems remain a vital and dynamic part of their IT infrastructure.

Chapter 2. Fundamentals of Mainframe Technology

In this chapter, we delve into the foundational aspects of mainframe technology. A thorough understanding of these fundamentals is crucial for grasping how modern automation techniques can be effectively applied.

2.1. Understanding Mainframe Architecture

Mainframe architecture is distinct and robust, designed to handle and process vast amounts of data with high reliability and availability. This section will break down the key components of mainframe architecture, including:

- **Central Processing Units (CPUs):** Unlike standard computers, mainframes often employ multiple CPUs for advanced parallel processing capabilities. We'll explore how these CPUs work together to handle large-scale transaction processing efficiently.
- **Storage Systems:** Mainframe storage solutions are unique, encompassing a range of storage media and technologies. We will examine hierarchical storage management, alongside the use of both internal and external storage systems, highlighting their relevance in maintaining the

speed and efficiency of mainframes.

- **Input/Output (I/O) Processing:** Mainframes handle an immense volume of I/O operations. This part will cover the sophisticated I/O processing mechanisms in mainframes, including channel subsystems and how they manage the vast data flow between the CPU, memory, and peripheral devices.
- **Networking:** Networking in mainframes, essential for connecting to various external systems and the internet, will be examined. The focus will be on the protocols and interfaces that enable mainframes to integrate seamlessly into organizational networks.

2.2. Mainframe Operating Systems: An Overview

Mainframe operating systems are specialized to maximize the utilization of hardware resources and provide a stable environment for running critical applications. Key topics to be covered here include:

- **Common Mainframe Operating Systems:** A look at popular mainframe operating systems like z/OS, z/VM, and Linux on IBM Z. Each of these operating systems offers different capabilities, from managing traditional mainframe applications to supporting modern open-source software.
- **Features and Capabilities:** We'll delve into the features that make these operating systems suitable for high-volume, mission-critical operations. This includes their multitasking abilities, security features, and support for complex, large-scale database and transaction processing systems.
- **System Management:** An exploration of how these

operating systems are managed, including aspects like system monitoring, workload management, and software updates.

2.3. Core Mainframe Applications and Uses

Mainframes are not just about powerful hardware and specialized operating systems; they are also about the applications and services they provide. This section will highlight:

- **Financial Services:** How mainframes handle high-volume transactions in banking, insurance, and stock exchanges, emphasizing their role in processing financial transactions, managing accounts, and ensuring data security.
- **Government and Public Sector:** The use of mainframes in managing public records, social security data, and other government services, underscoring their reliability and security in handling sensitive data.
- **Healthcare:** Examining how mainframes support healthcare systems, particularly in managing patient records, hospital management systems, and large-scale research data processing.
- **Retail and E-commerce:** The role of mainframes in supporting large retail and e-commerce platforms, especially in handling transactions, inventory management, and customer data processing.

Conclusion

The understanding of mainframe architecture, operating systems, and core applications lays the groundwork for comprehending their role in modern enterprises. This knowledge is essential for appreciating how automation can further enhance the efficiency and functionality of these powerful systems.

2.1. Understanding Mainframe Architecture

The architecture of mainframe computers sets them apart as the powerhouses of large-scale, mission-critical computing. This section delves into the key components that make up this architecture, explaining how each contributes to the overall performance and reliability of mainframes.

Central Processing Units (CPUs)

- **Parallel Processing Capabilities:** Mainframes often employ multiple CPUs, a stark contrast to standard computers. This parallel processing capability is crucial for handling large-scale transaction processing. We will explore how these CPUs, often working in a coordinated manner, handle vast workloads, distributing processing tasks to optimize efficiency and speed.
- **Advanced Computational Power:** Each CPU in a mainframe is designed for high throughput. The section will discuss the advanced computational power of these CPUs, which allows mainframes to execute complex transactions and operations at remarkable speeds.

Storage Systems

- **Hierarchical Storage Management:** Mainframe storage solutions are uniquely structured. Hierarchical Storage Management (HSM) is a critical component in this structure, allowing efficient data management across various storage media. We'll examine how HSM optimizes storage by automatically moving data between high-speed disk storage and slower, more cost-effective storage media, depending on the frequency of data access.
- **Internal and External Storage Systems:** The use of both internal and external storage systems in mainframes provides a blend of speed and capacity. This part will highlight the role of these storage systems in maintaining the speed and efficiency of mainframes, including how they handle vast volumes of data and ensure data availability and integrity.

Input/Output (I/O) Processing

- **Handling High Volume I/O Operations:** Mainframes are engineered to manage an immense volume of I/O operations, a critical aspect of their design. This section will cover the sophisticated I/O processing mechanisms in mainframes, which ensure that the data flow between CPUs, memory, and peripheral devices is managed efficiently.
- **Channel Subsystems:** The role of channel subsystems in managing I/O operations is central to mainframe architecture. We'll delve into how these subsystems handle the data flow, allowing for high-speed data transfer and processing, which is essential for the performance of mainframe systems.

Networking

- **Connectivity and Integration:** Networking in mainframes is essential for connecting to various external systems and the internet. This part of the section will focus on the networking capabilities of mainframes, including the protocols and interfaces used.
- **Seamless Integration into Organizational Networks:** The ability of mainframes to integrate seamlessly into organizational networks is critical for modern IT infrastructure. We'll explore how mainframes use various network technologies to ensure robust and secure connectivity, supporting a wide range of business applications.

Conclusion

Understanding the architecture of mainframes is fundamental to appreciating their role in modern computing environments. This robust architecture, with its advanced CPUs, specialized storage systems, sophisticated I/O processing mechanisms, and networking capabilities, is what makes mainframes uniquely suited for handling large-scale, critical operations in various industries.

2.2. Mainframe Operating Systems: An Overview

Mainframe operating systems are the linchpins that allow these powerful machines to efficiently utilize their hardware resources and provide a stable, secure environment for running a wide range of critical applications. This section offers an overview of the most common mainframe operating systems, their distinctive features and capabilities, and how they are managed to ensure optimal performance.

Common Mainframe Operating Systems

- **z/OS:** IBM's z/OS is one of the most widely used mainframe operating systems. Designed for robust performance, it is known for its reliability in managing traditional mainframe applications. This section will explore how z/OS supports large-scale transaction processing, complex database management, and high security, making it a preferred choice for many enterprises.
- **z/VM:** z/VM is another IBM offering, primarily known for its virtualization capabilities. It allows a single mainframe to run multiple operating system instances, making efficient use of system resources. We'll examine

how z/VM supports a range of applications and is particularly suited for consolidating workloads under one system.

- **Linux on IBM Z:** The integration of Linux with mainframe hardware, known as Linux on IBM Z, represents a shift towards open-source software on mainframes. This operating system brings the flexibility and innovation of the Linux ecosystem to the mainframe world. The section will highlight how Linux on IBM Z is used to run modern applications and services, bridging the gap between traditional mainframe processing and contemporary application demands.

Features and Capabilities

- **Multitasking Abilities:** Mainframe operating systems are renowned for their multitasking capabilities. This part will delve into how these systems efficiently handle numerous concurrent tasks, optimizing CPU usage and ensuring that resources are maximally utilized.
- **Security Features:** Security is paramount in mainframe environments, especially given the sensitive nature of the data they handle. We'll explore the advanced security features of mainframe operating systems, including access control mechanisms, encryption standards, and compliance with various security protocols.
- **Support for Large-Scale Databases and Transaction Systems:** The ability of mainframe operating systems to support complex, large-scale databases and transaction processing systems is a key feature. This section will illustrate how these systems manage vast amounts of data

with high throughput and reliability.

System Management

- **System Monitoring:** Effective system monitoring is crucial for the smooth operation of mainframes. We'll cover how these operating systems provide tools and utilities for real-time monitoring of system performance, resource utilization, and early detection of potential issues.
- **Workload Management:** Workload management capabilities ensure that the mainframe operates efficiently under varying load conditions. This section will discuss how mainframe operating systems prioritize and manage workloads, maintaining optimal performance even under high demand.
- **Software Updates and Maintenance:** Keeping mainframe operating systems up-to-date and well-maintained is essential. We'll explore the processes involved in updating these systems, including patch management and the deployment of new features, ensuring that they stay secure and functional.

Conclusion

Mainframe operating systems are sophisticated platforms that underpin the functionality of these computing giants. Understanding these operating systems, from their core features to their management, is essential for anyone looking to leverage the full potential of mainframe technology in an automated and modern computing environment.

2.3. Core Mainframe Applications and Uses

Mainframes are much more than their robust hardware and specialized operating systems. They are the powerhouses behind many critical applications and services across various industries. This section highlights the pivotal role of mainframes in key sectors, underscoring their unmatched capabilities in handling large-scale, critical operations.

Financial Services

- **High-Volume Transactions in Banking:** Mainframes are the backbone of the banking industry, processing millions of transactions daily. This includes everything from ATM withdrawals to complex financial trades. We'll explore how mainframes handle these transactions with high efficiency and accuracy, ensuring seamless financial operations.
- **Insurance and Stock Exchanges:** In the world of insurance and stock exchanges, mainframes play a critical role in managing vast amounts of data and transactions. Their ability to process high volumes of transactions while ensuring data integrity and security is unparalleled, making them indispensable in these sectors.
- **Data Security and Account Management:** One of the

most significant aspects of mainframes in financial services is their robust security capabilities, crucial for protecting sensitive financial data. This section will discuss how mainframes manage and secure customer accounts and transaction data, complying with stringent regulatory standards.

Government and Public Sector

- **Managing Public Records:** Mainframes are extensively used in the public sector to manage large public records, from census data to tax records. Their ability to handle and store vast amounts of data securely makes them ideal for these applications.
- **Social Security Data:** In managing social security data, mainframes offer the necessary reliability and security. We'll delve into how these systems support the complex needs of social security administration, including record keeping, payment processing, and data protection.
- **Other Government Services:** This part will also touch on the use of mainframes in other government services, such as licensing, public safety, and utility management, highlighting their role in efficient public administration.

Healthcare

- **Patient Records and Hospital Management:** Mainframes support healthcare systems by managing extensive patient records and hospital management systems. Their capacity for handling large-scale data processing and maintaining high levels of confidentiality is vital in this sensitive sector.
- **Large-Scale Research Data Processing:** Mainframes

facilitate significant research efforts in healthcare, processing vast datasets for medical research. This capability is crucial for advancements in medical science, where processing large volumes of data is a routine requirement.

Retail and E-commerce

- **Transaction Processing:** In retail and e-commerce, mainframes process countless transactions. This section will illustrate how they handle sales transactions, inventory updates, and customer interactions, ensuring a smooth retail operation.
- **Inventory Management and Customer Data Processing:** The role of mainframes in managing inventory and processing customer data is critical for the efficiency of retail and e-commerce platforms. We'll examine how these systems provide the scalability and reliability needed to manage fluctuating demands and large customer databases.

Conclusion

Mainframes play a crucial role in the smooth functioning of numerous industries. From financial services to healthcare, they underpin many of the essential services that form the backbone of modern society. Understanding these applications and uses is key to appreciating the continued relevance and importance of mainframe technology in today's digital world.

Chapter 3. Principles of Automation

In this chapter, we transition from the foundational aspects of mainframe technology to the principles of automation. Understanding these principles is crucial for effectively implementing and managing automation in mainframe environments.

3.1. Introduction to Automation Concepts

Automation in the context of information technology refers to the use of systems or software to perform tasks that would otherwise require manual intervention. This section will introduce the fundamental concepts of automation, including:

- **Definition and Scope:** A comprehensive definition of automation, covering its scope in various IT processes. This includes everything from simple scripted tasks to complex operations managed by AI and ML.
- **History and Evolution:** A brief history of automation in computing, tracing its evolution from basic batch scripts to sophisticated AI-driven processes. This perspective helps in understanding how automation has become an integral part of modern computing.
- **Benefits of Automation:** An exploration of the benefits of

automation, such as increased efficiency, reduced human error, and the ability to perform complex computations and data analysis at scale.

3.2. Differentiating Between Traditional and Modern Automation

The landscape of automation has undergone significant changes over the years. This section will distinguish between traditional and modern automation approaches:

- **Traditional Automation:** An overview of traditional automation methods, including scheduled batch processing and rule-based automation. This part will discuss how these methods were initially used in mainframes and other computing systems.
- **Modern Automation Techniques:** An exploration of modern automation techniques, like RPA, AI, and ML. This section will illustrate how these advanced technologies offer more dynamic and intelligent automation capabilities compared to traditional methods.
- **Transition from Traditional to Modern Automation:** A discussion on the transition process from traditional to modern automation, highlighting the challenges and opportunities that this shift presents.

3.3. Key Principles of Effective Automation

Effective automation requires more than just the implementation of technology; it demands a strategic approach. This section will delve into the key principles of effective automation:

- **Strategic Planning and Goal Setting:** Outlining the

importance of strategic planning in automation, including setting clear goals and objectives. This planning ensures that automation efforts align with business needs and deliver tangible benefits.

- **Integration with Existing Systems:** A guide to integrating automation solutions with existing systems, particularly focusing on how modern automation tools can be incorporated into mainframe environments without disrupting their operations.
- **Scalability and Flexibility:** Discussing the importance of scalability and flexibility in automation. As business needs evolve, automation solutions must be able to adapt and scale accordingly.
- **Monitoring and Continuous Improvement:** Highlighting the need for ongoing monitoring of automation systems to ensure they are functioning as intended and to identify areas for improvement. Continuous improvement is essential to maximize the benefits of automation over time.
- **Skill Development and Change Management:** Addressing the human aspect of automation, including the need for skill development and effective change management practices to ensure a smooth transition and adoption of automated processes.

Conclusion

Understanding the principles of automation is key to leveraging its full potential in mainframe environments and beyond. This foundational knowledge sets the stage for the following chapters, which will delve into the specifics of applying these principles in the context of mainframe automation.

3.1. Introduction to Automation Concepts

In the realm of information technology, automation stands as a cornerstone concept, revolutionizing how tasks and processes are executed. This section introduces the fundamental concepts of automation, defining its scope, tracing its historical development, and highlighting its manifold benefits.

Definition and Scope

- **Comprehensive Definition:** Automation, in the IT context, refers to the use of various systems and software applications to perform tasks that traditionally required manual intervention. This broad definition encompasses a wide range of activities, from straightforward scripted tasks to highly complex operations managed through advanced technologies like Artificial Intelligence (AI) and Machine Learning (ML).
- **Scope in IT Processes:** The scope of automation in IT is extensive and multifaceted. It includes automating routine data entry jobs, complex network management, system monitoring tasks, and even decision-making processes that rely on data analytics and pattern recognition. Automation's versatility lies in its ability to be applied

across various levels of IT operations, catering to simple repetitive tasks as well as to sophisticated analytical processes.

History and Evolution

- **From Batch Scripts to AI-Driven Processes:** The history of automation in computing is a progressive narrative that begins with basic batch scripts. These scripts were designed to automate simple repetitive tasks, reducing the need for manual input. Over time, as technological capabilities advanced, so did the scope and complexity of automation. The advent of AI and ML has further propelled this evolution, enabling automation to handle not just repetitive tasks, but also complex decision-making processes that adapt and learn from data.
- **Milestones in Automation Evolution:** Key milestones in this evolution will be highlighted, such as the development of early programming languages, the introduction of operating systems with built-in automation capabilities, and the rise of AI and ML in recent years, which have significantly expanded the possibilities of what can be automated.

Benefits of Automation

- **Increased Efficiency and Productivity:** One of the primary benefits of automation is the significant increase in efficiency and productivity it brings. Automated systems can operate continuously without fatigue, handling large volumes of tasks at speeds unmatchable by human effort.
- **Reduction in Human Error:** By automating tasks,

especially repetitive and mundane ones, the likelihood of errors commonly associated with human intervention is greatly reduced. This leads to higher accuracy and reliability in processes and outcomes.

- **Complex Computations and Data Analysis:** Automation enables the handling of complex computations and large-scale data analysis, which are beyond human capacity to perform manually. This aspect is particularly beneficial in fields where data-driven insights are crucial for decision-making.
- **Scalability and Consistency:** Automation allows for the scalability of operations while maintaining consistency in performance. It enables businesses and organizations to handle growing workloads without compromising on the quality or speed of their services.

Conclusion

The introduction to automation concepts underscores its pivotal role in transforming the IT landscape. From simple beginnings to its current state where AI and ML redefine its capabilities, automation has become an integral component of modern computing, offering a multitude of benefits that enhance efficiency, accuracy, and the overall effectiveness of IT processes.

Definition and Scope

Comprehensive Definition

Automation, within the context of information technology (IT), signifies the utilization of diverse systems and software applications to execute tasks that traditionally necessitated manual intervention. This definition captures a vast spectrum of activities:

- **Simplistic Scripted Tasks:** At its most basic, automation in IT involves scripting routine tasks. These can range from automating the start-up and shut-down of systems to running scheduled data backups. Scripts act as set instructions for computers to perform these tasks consistently and without the need for human oversight.
- **Complex Operations with AI and ML:** At the more advanced end, automation encompasses intricate operations managed by cutting-edge technologies like Artificial Intelligence (AI) and Machine Learning (ML). Here, automation transcends basic task execution to include adaptive processes that can learn from data, make predictions, or optimize operations based on complex algorithms.

Scope in IT Processes

The scope of automation in IT is both extensive and varied, covering a multitude of processes and functions:

- **Routine Data Entry and Processing:** Automation plays a vital role in simplifying mundane tasks such as data entry, where it not only increases efficiency but also minimizes errors commonly associated with manual input.
- **Complex Network Management:** In the realm of network management, automation contributes to the

monitoring and maintenance of complex network infrastructures, ensuring optimal performance and quick response to issues.

- **System Monitoring Tasks:** Automated monitoring systems keep a vigilant eye on IT infrastructures, preemptively identifying and addressing potential issues, from server overloads to security breaches, thereby maintaining system health and security.
- **Decision-Making Based on Data Analytics:** Perhaps most significantly, automation has carved a niche in decision-making processes. By leveraging data analytics and pattern recognition, automated systems can provide insights and make informed decisions, which are particularly crucial in areas like market analysis, financial forecasting, and strategic planning.
- **Versatility Across IT Operations:** The versatility of automation is evident in its applicability across various levels of IT operations. Whether it's executing simple repetitive tasks or engaging in complex analytical processes, automation has the capability to enhance efficiency, accuracy, and overall effectiveness.

History and Evolution

From Batch Scripts to AI-Driven Processes

The history of automation in computing is a tale of continual progression and sophistication. This journey can be traced back to the inception of batch scripts, marking the early days of automation.

- **The Era of Batch Scripts:** Initially, automation in computing was synonymous with batch scripting. These scripts were designed to automate simple, repetitive tasks, such as data backups or batch processing of transactions. The primary goal was to reduce manual intervention, increase efficiency, and minimize the risk of human error.
- **Increasing Complexity and Capability:** As technology advanced, so did the scope and complexity of automation. From simple scripts, automation evolved to encompass more complex tasks, involving intricate sequences of operations and decision-making processes.
- **The Advent of AI and ML:** The introduction of Artificial Intelligence (AI) and Machine Learning (ML) marked a significant leap in the evolution of automation. These technologies enabled systems to not just perform predefined tasks but also to adapt and learn from data. Automation, thus, transitioned from being task-oriented to becoming data-driven and intelligence-based.

Milestones in Automation Evolution

- **Development of Early Programming Languages:** The creation of early programming languages was a pivotal moment in automation history. These languages, like COBOL and FORTRAN, laid the groundwork for more sophisticated automated processes, allowing for more complex tasks to be encoded and executed.

- **Introduction of Operating Systems with Built-in Automation Capabilities:** The emergence of operating systems equipped with built-in automation features further propelled the evolution. These operating systems enabled more advanced scheduling and management of tasks, streamlining the operation of computer systems.
- **Rise of AI and ML:** The rise of AI and ML in recent years has been a game-changer. These technologies have expanded the boundaries of what can be automated, moving beyond routine tasks to encompass areas like predictive analytics, natural language processing, and even autonomous decision-making.
- **Expanding Automation Across Industries:** Another significant milestone is the expansion of automation across various industries. From manufacturing and finance to healthcare and retail, automation has become an integral part of operational strategies, driving efficiency, innovation, and competitive advantage.

Conclusion

The evolution of automation in computing reflects the broader narrative of technological advancement. From its humble beginnings with batch scripts to the current landscape dominated by AI and ML, automation has continuously evolved, reshaping the way tasks and processes are executed in the IT domain.

Benefits of Automation

The adoption of automation in various sectors of the IT industry has brought about a multitude of benefits. These advantages have not only transformed operational efficiencies but have also opened new avenues for innovation and growth.

Increased Efficiency and Productivity

- **Continuous Operation:** One of the most significant benefits of automation is the dramatic increase in efficiency and productivity. Automated systems can operate around the clock without the limitations of human fatigue. This continuous operation is particularly crucial in environments that require constant monitoring or in processing tasks that are time-sensitive.
- **Handling Large Volumes of Tasks:** Automation excels in managing large volumes of tasks, often at speeds that are unattainable by human efforts. This capability is especially beneficial in data-intensive fields such as big data analytics and mass transaction processing, where the volume of work would be unmanageable for human workers.

Reduction in Human Error

- **Consistency and Accuracy:** Automation significantly reduces the likelihood of errors, particularly in repetitive and routine tasks. Human error, while a natural part of manual processes, can lead to inconsistencies and inaccuracies. Automated systems, governed by predefined rules and algorithms, maintain a consistent level of accuracy and reliability.
- **Improved Process Outcomes:** The reduction in human error directly contributes to higher quality outcomes. In

environments where precision is paramount, such as in financial calculations or data entry, the precision offered by automation is invaluable.

Complex Computations and Data Analysis

- **Handling Sophisticated Operations:** Automation has the capability to handle complex computations and conduct large-scale data analysis that would be beyond the scope of manual human capacity. This ability is crucial in sectors where advanced data analysis and complex computational models are the norm.
- **Data-Driven Decision Making:** In fields where decision-making relies heavily on data analysis, such as market research, logistics, and healthcare, automation provides the tools to gather, process, and analyze vast datasets, enabling more informed and timely decisions.

Scalability and Consistency

- **Adapting to Growing Workloads:** Automation offers scalability, allowing businesses and organizations to expand their operations without a proportional increase in labor or resources. This scalability is vital in responding to growing workloads or expanding service offerings.
- **Uniform Performance:** Another key benefit of automation is the consistency it brings to operations. Unlike human performance, which can vary due to numerous factors, automated systems maintain a uniform level of performance, ensuring consistent quality in services and products.

Conclusion

The benefits of automation in IT are clear and impactful. From increased efficiency and productivity to enhanced accuracy and the ability to perform complex tasks, automation has become a fundamental component in the modern digital landscape. Its role in ensuring scalability and consistency further underscores its value across various sectors and applications.

3.2. Differentiating Between Traditional and Modern Automation

The evolution of automation in the IT sector is a story of continuous advancement, marked by a shift from traditional methods to more dynamic and intelligent modern techniques. This section explores the differences between these two approaches, their applications, and the transition from one to the other.

Traditional Automation

- **Scheduled Batch Processing:** One of the cornerstones of traditional automation is scheduled batch processing. This method involves accumulating data over a period and then processing it all at once, typically during off-peak hours. In mainframes and early computing systems, this was an efficient way to handle large volumes of data without impacting day-to-day operations.
- **Rule-Based Automation:** Traditional automation also heavily relied on rule-based systems. These systems execute tasks based on a set of predefined rules. For example, a rule might dictate that if a certain condition is met, a specific action should be taken. This form of automation was

straightforward but lacked flexibility and adaptability.

Modern Automation Techniques

- **Robotic Process Automation (RPA):** RPA represents a significant leap in the field of automation. It involves the use of software robots or 'bots' to automate routine tasks that mimic human actions. Unlike traditional automation, RPA is non-invasive and interacts with systems at the interface level, making it more versatile and easier to implement.
- **Artificial Intelligence (AI) and Machine Learning (ML):** AI and ML bring a level of intelligence to automation that was previously unattainable. AI enables machines to simulate human intelligence processes, while ML allows them to learn from data and improve over time. Together, they enable automation systems to handle complex tasks, make predictions, and adapt to changing scenarios.

Transition from Traditional to Modern Automation

- **Challenges in Transition:** The shift from traditional to modern automation has not been without challenges. One significant hurdle is the integration of modern automation tools with legacy systems. There's also the challenge of upskilling the workforce to handle these advanced technologies.
- **Opportunities Presented:** Despite these challenges, the transition presents numerous opportunities. Modern automation techniques can significantly increase efficiency, reduce costs, and open up new possibilities for innovation

and service improvement. They offer a level of flexibility and scalability that traditional methods cannot match.

- **Strategies for Effective Transition:** An effective transition strategy involves a phased approach, starting with areas where the most immediate benefits can be realized. It also requires investment in training and development to equip the workforce with the necessary skills.

Conclusion

The transition from traditional to modern automation marks a significant shift in the capabilities of IT systems. While traditional methods laid the groundwork, modern techniques like RPA, AI, and ML are transforming the landscape, offering more sophisticated, flexible, and intelligent automation solutions.

Traditional Automation

In the realm of computing, traditional automation has been a foundational element, especially in the era of mainframes and early computing systems. This section delves into the key components of traditional automation: scheduled batch processing and rule-based automation.

Scheduled Batch Processing

- **Concept and Application:** Scheduled batch processing is a method where data is accumulated over a period and then processed collectively, typically during off-peak hours. This approach was particularly advantageous in early computing environments where processing power and resources were limited compared to today's standards.
- **Efficiency in Mainframes:** In the context of mainframes, scheduled batch processing was an essential technique. It allowed for the efficient handling of large volumes of data, such as financial transactions or inventory updates, without overloading the system during operational hours. This method ensured that critical day-to-day operations of businesses were not interrupted while still processing necessary data.
- **Operational Workflow:** The typical workflow involved collecting data throughout the day, scheduling processing tasks during non-peak hours, and then updating systems with the processed data. This cycle was crucial in maintaining the continuity and efficiency of business operations.

Rule-Based Automation

- **Mechanism of Operation:** Rule-based automation

operates on a simple yet effective principle: if certain predefined conditions are met, specified actions are triggered. These rules are explicit, with clear conditions and corresponding actions.

- **Applications and Limitations:** This form of automation was widely used for tasks such as system monitoring, where specific system states would trigger alerts or actions, and in transaction processing systems, where certain transaction types would initiate predefined procedures. While rule-based automation provided a level of reliability and predictability, it lacked the flexibility to adapt to changing scenarios or handle complex, non-linear tasks.
- **Structure and Reliability:** The straightforward nature of rule-based systems made them relatively easy to implement and manage. They were known for their reliability, as the outcome of a given input was predictable and consistent. However, the rigidity of these systems meant that any change in processes or introduction of new variables required extensive reconfiguration.

Conclusion

Traditional automation, with its scheduled batch processing and rule-based systems, laid the groundwork for the automation technologies we see today. Understanding these foundational elements is crucial in appreciating the evolution of automation in computing and recognizing the limitations that modern automation seeks to overcome.

Modern Automation Techniques

The landscape of automation has been revolutionized by the advent of modern techniques like Robotic Process Automation (RPA), Artificial Intelligence (AI), and Machine Learning (ML). These technologies represent a significant shift from traditional automation methods, offering greater flexibility, intelligence, and adaptability.

Robotic Process Automation (RPA)

- **Definition and Functionality:** RPA involves the use of software robots, or 'bots', to automate routine and repetitive tasks that typically require human intervention. These tasks range from data entry and extraction to complex workflow operations.
- **Non-Invasive Nature:** One of the key features of RPA is its non-invasive nature. RPA bots operate at the interface level, meaning they can interact with existing systems and applications without the need for extensive modifications. This attribute makes RPA highly versatile and easier to implement compared to traditional automation methods.
- **Mimicking Human Actions:** RPA bots are designed to mimic human actions. They can log into applications, move files, fill in forms, extract data, and perform a wide range of rule-based tasks, just as a human worker would do.
- **Benefits:** The primary benefits of RPA include increased efficiency, reduced error rates, and the ability to free up human employees to focus on more complex, value-added tasks. RPA is particularly useful in sectors like banking, insurance, and healthcare, where large volumes of data handling are required.

Artificial Intelligence (AI) and Machine Learning (ML)

- **Advanced Intelligence in Automation:** AI and ML introduce a level of intelligence to automation that was previously unattainable. AI refers to the simulation of human intelligence in machines, programmed to think and learn like humans. ML, a subset of AI, involves the ability of these systems to automatically learn and improve from experience without being explicitly programmed.
- **Complex Task Handling and Predictive Analysis:** AI and ML enable automation systems to handle complex tasks that require decision-making and problem-solving abilities. They are also used in predictive analysis, where the system can analyze data, identify patterns, and make informed predictions or decisions based on that analysis.
- **Adaptability:** One of the most significant advantages of AI and ML in automation is their adaptability. These technologies allow systems to adapt to new information or changes in the environment, making them ideal for dynamic and evolving business landscapes.
- **Applications:** The applications of AI and ML in automation are vast, ranging from customer service chatbots and virtual assistants to sophisticated data analytics and fraud detection systems in financial services.

Conclusion

Modern automation techniques like RPA, AI, and ML have transformed the field of automation. They have expanded the capabilities of automated systems from simple task execution to complex problem-solving and decision-making. This evolution not only enhances operational efficiencies but also opens up new possibilities for innovation and strategic advancements in various industries.

Transition from Traditional to Modern Automation

The transition from traditional to modern automation techniques represents a significant shift in the IT landscape. While this shift offers numerous benefits, it is not without its challenges and requires strategic planning to navigate effectively.

Challenges in Transition

- **Integration with Legacy Systems:** One of the primary challenges in transitioning to modern automation is integrating new technologies with existing legacy systems. These older systems often have complex, deeply embedded processes that are not readily compatible with new automation tools, making integration a delicate and sometimes challenging process.
- **Upskilling the Workforce:** Another significant challenge is the need for upskilling the existing workforce. Modern automation technologies like AI and ML require a certain level of expertise and understanding. Ensuring that the workforce is adequately trained to handle these advanced technologies is crucial for a smooth transition.
- **Cultural and Organizational Hurdles:** Often overlooked are the cultural and organizational changes that come with adopting new technologies. Resistance to change, adapting to new workflows, and redefining job roles can be significant hurdles in the transition process.

Opportunities Presented

- **Increased Efficiency and Cost Reduction:** Modern automation technologies offer a significant increase in operational efficiency and the potential for considerable cost savings. By automating routine tasks, organizations can redirect resources and focus on more strategic areas.

- **Innovation and Service Improvement:** The advanced capabilities of modern automation open up new avenues for innovation. They enable organizations to develop new services or improve existing ones, enhancing competitiveness and customer satisfaction.
- **Flexibility and Scalability:** Modern automation offers a level of flexibility and scalability that traditional methods cannot match. It allows organizations to adapt quickly to changing market demands and scale operations as needed.

Strategies for Effective Transition

- **Phased Approach:** A phased approach to transitioning is often most effective. This involves starting with areas where the most immediate benefits can be realized, which helps in demonstrating the value of modern automation and building momentum for further implementation.
- **Investment in Training and Development:** To address the skills gap, substantial investment in training and development is essential. This not only equips the workforce with the necessary skills but also helps in easing the cultural transition to a more automated environment.
- **Strategic Planning:** Aligning the transition with the organization's strategic objectives is crucial. This includes identifying key areas for automation, assessing the impact on current processes and systems, and planning for the integration of new technologies in a way that supports the organization's long-term goals.

Conclusion

The transition from traditional to modern automation is a journey that requires careful planning, a strategic approach, and a willingness to invest in new skills and technologies. Despite the challenges, the opportunities it presents are vast, offering organizations the chance to enhance efficiency, foster innovation, and remain competitive in an increasingly digital world.

3.3. Key Principles of Effective Automation

Effective automation is not merely about deploying technology; it's about a strategic approach that aligns with an organization's goals and adapts to its evolving needs. This section explores the fundamental principles that underpin successful automation initiatives.

Strategic Planning and Goal Setting

- **Aligning Automation with Business Objectives:** The cornerstone of effective automation is strategic planning that aligns with the overarching business objectives. Clear goals and objectives should be set for what the automation efforts are intended to achieve, whether it's cost reduction, efficiency improvement, quality enhancement, or innovation.
- **Setting Measurable Goals:** Goals for automation should be specific, measurable, achievable, relevant, and time-bound (SMART). This ensures that the impact of automation can be effectively measured and evaluated against business objectives.

Integration with Existing Systems

- **Seamless Integration Strategies:** A critical aspect of effective automation is the ability to integrate new tools and technologies with existing systems, especially in mainframe environments. This integration should be seamless, ensuring that automation tools complement and enhance existing operations without causing disruptions.
- **Customization and Compatibility:** Automation solutions should be chosen and customized based on their compatibility with existing systems. The aim is to create a cohesive ecosystem where old and new systems work in harmony.

Scalability and Flexibility

- **Adaptable to Changing Business Needs:** Automation solutions must be scalable and flexible to accommodate future business growth and changing market conditions. This involves choosing technologies that can be scaled up or down based on demand and can be modified as business processes evolve.
- **Modular and Agile Approaches:** Adopting modular and agile approaches in automation helps in managing scalability. This allows businesses to expand or modify their automation capabilities in a controlled and efficient manner.

Monitoring and Continuous Improvement

- **Ongoing Evaluation:** Continuous monitoring of automation systems is essential to ensure they are functioning as intended. This includes regular checks for efficiency, accuracy, and performance.

- **Iterative Improvement Process:** Automation should be seen as an ongoing process that involves regular updates and improvements. Feedback loops and analytics play a crucial role in identifying areas for enhancement and ensuring the automation system evolves to deliver maximum value.

Skill Development and Change Management

- **Investment in Training:** As automation technologies evolve, so does the need for skill development. Investing in training and upskilling the workforce is crucial for the effective management and maintenance of automation systems.
- **Effective Change Management:** The human aspect of automation is often the most challenging. Effective change management practices are essential to address concerns, manage resistance, and ensure a smooth transition to automated processes.

Conclusion

The principles of effective automation highlight the need for a strategic, integrated, and flexible approach, underpinned by continuous monitoring and improvement. Equally important is the focus on people, through skill development and change management, to ensure successful adoption and optimization of automation technologies.

Strategic Planning and Goal Setting

For automation to be truly effective and deliver its full potential, it must be rooted in strategic planning and goal setting. This approach ensures that automation initiatives are in line with the broader business objectives and contribute meaningfully to organizational success.

Aligning Automation with Business Objectives

- **Understanding Business Needs:** The first step in strategic planning for automation is to thoroughly understand the business's overarching goals and challenges. This understanding helps in identifying areas where automation can have the most significant impact.
- **Defining Clear Objectives:** Once the needs are understood, the next step is to define clear objectives for the automation project. These objectives should directly support the broader business goals. For instance, if a business aims to enhance customer satisfaction, automation efforts could focus on streamlining customer service processes.
- **Holistic Approach:** Effective automation should not be implemented in isolation. It should be considered as part of a holistic strategy that encompasses technology, people, and processes. This approach ensures that automation efforts are integrated smoothly into the existing business ecosystem.

Setting Measurable Goals

- **SMART Goals:** Setting goals for automation using the SMART criteria (Specific, Measurable, Achievable, Relevant, and Time-bound) is essential. For example, a specific goal might be to reduce the time for processing customer inquiries by 30% within six months using RPA.

- **Quantifiable Metrics:** To measure the effectiveness of automation, it's important to establish quantifiable metrics. These could include metrics like process completion time, error rates, cost savings, or customer satisfaction scores.
- **Regular Review and Adjustment:** Goals should not be static; they need regular review and adjustment based on the evolving business environment and the results obtained from initial automation efforts. This adaptive approach ensures that the automation strategy remains aligned with business objectives.
- **Stakeholder Involvement:** Involving stakeholders in the goal-setting process ensures that the objectives of automation are aligned with the needs and expectations of different departments and teams within the organization.

Conclusion

Strategic planning and goal setting are fundamental to the success of any automation initiative. By aligning automation with business objectives and setting SMART goals, organizations can ensure that their investment in automation delivers tangible benefits and drives their business forward.

Integration with Existing Systems

Integrating automation seamlessly into existing systems is a critical step in ensuring the success and effectiveness of any automation initiative. This is especially true in environments with established mainframe systems, where the integration must be handled with precision and foresight.

Seamless Integration Strategies

- **Assessment and Planning:** The first step in achieving seamless integration is a thorough assessment of the existing systems. Understanding the current infrastructure, including its capabilities and limitations, is crucial. Based on this assessment, a detailed integration plan should be developed, outlining how the new automation tools will interface with the existing systems.
- **Middleware and APIs:** Utilizing middleware and application programming interfaces (APIs) can facilitate smooth integration. These technologies act as bridges between new automation tools and existing systems, enabling them to communicate and work together effectively.
- **Minimizing Disruption:** The integration process should be designed to minimize disruption to ongoing operations. This might involve phased implementation or running parallel systems temporarily to ensure continuity of operations.
- **Testing and Validation:** Rigorous testing is essential to ensure that the integrated system functions as intended. This should include testing for performance, scalability, and security to validate the integration before full-scale deployment.

Customization and Compatibility

- **Choosing the Right Tools:** Selecting automation tools and technologies that are inherently compatible with existing systems is vital. This compatibility simplifies the integration process and reduces the likelihood of conflicts or performance issues.
- **Customization for Cohesion:** Often, off-the-shelf automation solutions will need to be customized to fit seamlessly into the existing technological environment. Customization should be done keeping in mind the unique requirements of the current systems and the specific objectives of the automation initiative.
- **Building a Cohesive Ecosystem:** The ultimate goal is to create a cohesive ecosystem where old and new systems work in harmony. This integration should not only enhance current capabilities but also lay a foundation for future scalability and upgrades.
- **Continuous Monitoring and Adjustment:** Post-integration, continuous monitoring is crucial to ensure the systems operate harmoniously. Feedback mechanisms should be in place to identify any issues and make adjustments as needed.

Conclusion

Effective integration of automation tools with existing systems is a meticulous process that requires careful planning, selection of compatible tools, and ongoing monitoring. When executed well, it ensures that automation enhances and complements existing operations, leading to a more efficient and productive environment.

Scalability and Flexibility

In an ever-changing business landscape, the scalability and flexibility of automation solutions are paramount. The ability to adapt and scale these solutions is crucial for businesses to stay competitive and responsive to market demands.

Adaptable to Changing Business Needs

- **Choosing Scalable Technologies:** When selecting automation technologies, it's essential to consider their scalability. Scalable solutions can handle increasing loads or transaction volumes without a significant drop in performance. This could involve technologies that offer cloud-based services, which are inherently scalable, or software that can easily be upgraded to handle more complex tasks.
- **Flexibility in Automation:** Flexibility is equally important. The chosen automation solutions should be adaptable to changing business processes and able to integrate with new technologies as they emerge. This means opting for solutions with open standards, customizable workflows, and the ability to integrate with a variety of systems and platforms.
- **Anticipating Future Growth:** Planning for automation should include a roadmap that anticipates future business growth and technological advancements. This ensures that the automation strategy remains relevant and effective in the long term.

Modular and Agile Approaches

- **Modular Automation Systems:** Implementing modular automation systems is a strategic approach to scalability and flexibility. Modular systems allow components or functionalities to be added, removed, or modified without disrupting the entire system. This approach provides businesses with the agility to respond quickly to new opportunities or challenges.

- **Agile Methodology in Automation:** Adopting an agile methodology in deploying automation can facilitate continuous improvement and adaptation. In an agile environment, automation solutions are implemented in iterative cycles, allowing for regular feedback and adjustments. This ensures that the automation remains aligned with business goals and can evolve with changing needs.
- **Benefits of a Modular and Agile Approach:** The modular and agile approaches allow for incremental enhancements and adjustments, reducing the risks associated with large-scale changes. They also enable businesses to experiment with new automation technologies on a smaller scale before wider implementation.

Conclusion

Scalability and flexibility are critical attributes for effective automation, ensuring that solutions remain efficient and relevant over time. By focusing on scalable, flexible, and modular automation strategies, businesses can ensure that their automation investments continue to deliver value in the face of changing market dynamics and business needs.

Monitoring and Continuous Improvement

In the dynamic world of automation, ongoing evaluation and iterative improvement are key to ensuring that automation systems continually meet and exceed performance expectations. This ongoing process is crucial for maintaining the relevance and efficiency of automated operations.

Ongoing Evaluation

- **Regular Performance Checks:** Continuous monitoring of automation systems involves regular checks for efficiency, accuracy, and overall performance. This ensures that the systems are functioning as intended and delivering the expected benefits.
- **Metrics and KPIs:** Establishing clear metrics and key performance indicators (KPIs) is essential for effective monitoring. These metrics might include process completion times, error rates, system uptime, and user satisfaction levels. They provide quantifiable data that can be used to assess the performance of the automation systems.
- **Proactive Issue Resolution:** Continuous monitoring allows for the early detection of issues, enabling proactive resolution before they escalate into bigger problems. This includes monitoring for system anomalies, performance bottlenecks, and other irregularities that might indicate underlying issues.

Iterative Improvement Process

- **Feedback Loops:** Implementing feedback loops is crucial in the automation lifecycle. Feedback, whether from system users, performance metrics, or error logs, should be used to inform improvements in the system. This feedback can help identify areas that are not performing as expected or where user needs have changed.

- **Regular Updates and Enhancements:** Automation should be viewed as an evolving process, with regular updates and improvements based on the feedback received. This could involve tweaking algorithms, updating software, or even reengineering processes to better align with business goals.
- **Leveraging Analytics:** Advanced analytics play a significant role in continuous improvement. By analyzing data generated by automation systems, organizations can gain insights into performance trends, potential areas for optimization, and opportunities for further automation.
- **Agile Methodology:** Employing an agile approach to managing automation projects can facilitate continuous improvement. This involves iterative development cycles, where improvements are made in small increments, allowing for more flexible and responsive enhancements.

Conclusion

Monitoring and continuous improvement are indispensable in the lifecycle of automation. By continuously evaluating and iteratively improving automation systems, organizations can ensure that they remain efficient, effective, and aligned with evolving business needs.

Skill Development and Change Management

The successful implementation of automation not only hinges on the technology itself but also on the people who manage and interact with it. Skill development and effective change management are crucial components of this process.

Investment in Training

- **Addressing the Skills Gap:** As automation technologies become more sophisticated, the skill sets required to manage them evolve. There is often a gap between the capabilities of the current workforce and the skills needed to effectively operate and maintain new automation systems. Closing this gap requires a targeted investment in training and upskilling.
- **Customized Training Programs:** Developing customized training programs that cater to the specific needs of the workforce and the nuances of the implemented automation solutions is vital. This could include training on specific automation tools, programming languages, system maintenance, and data analysis.
- **Continuous Learning:** Skill development in the field of automation should be viewed as a continuous journey. As technologies evolve, ongoing learning opportunities should be provided to keep the workforce up-to-date with the latest developments.
- **Empowering Employees:** Training should not only focus on technical skills but also empower employees to understand the strategic importance of automation in their roles and the broader business context. This helps in creating a workforce that is not just capable but also motivated to leverage automation effectively.

Effective Change Management

- **Addressing Human Resistance:** One of the primary challenges in implementing automation is managing the human response to change. Concerns about job displacement, fear of the unknown, and discomfort with new technologies can lead to resistance.
- **Communicating the Change:** Effective communication is key in managing this resistance. This involves clearly articulating the reasons for automation, how it will impact the workforce, and the benefits it will bring to the organization and its employees.
- **Inclusive Approach:** Involving employees in the automation process from the outset can help in mitigating resistance. This could be through collaborative planning, soliciting feedback, or involving them in decision-making processes related to automation.
- **Support Systems:** Establishing support systems, such as help desks or mentoring programs, can assist employees in adapting to new systems and processes. Emotional and psychological support can also play a crucial role in easing the transition.

Conclusion

Skill development and change management are critical to the successful implementation and sustainability of automation initiatives. By investing in training and managing the human aspect of change effectively, organizations can not only enhance the efficiency of their automation systems but also foster a culture that embraces continuous improvement and innovation.

Chapter 4. Modern Automation Tools and Technologies

In this chapter, we delve into the heart of modern automation by exploring the tools and technologies that are reshaping mainframe environments. From the sophistication of AI and ML to the expansive capabilities of cloud computing, we will uncover how these advancements are revolutionizing the automation landscape.

4.1. Overview of Automation Tools

This section provides a comprehensive overview of the various tools that are integral to modern automation. We will examine a range of solutions from basic task automation tools to more complex systems that integrate various aspects of AI, ML, and data analytics.

- **Task Automation Tools:** We will begin with an exploration of task automation tools which are used to automate routine tasks such as data entry, batch processing, and system monitoring.
- **Robotic Process Automation (RPA):** A deeper look into RPA tools will reveal how they are used to replicate human actions and automate repetitive tasks in a non-invasive manner.
- **Workflow Automation Platforms:** These platforms are

crucial for automating and optimizing business processes. We'll explore how they help in streamlining workflows, enhancing efficiency, and reducing manual errors.

- **API-Based Automation:** The role of APIs in automation, particularly in integrating different systems and enabling them to work together seamlessly, will also be discussed.

4.2. Leveraging AI and Machine Learning in Mainframe Automation

AI and ML are at the forefront of transforming mainframe automation. This section will delve into how these technologies are being integrated into mainframe environments and the benefits they bring.

- **AI in Predictive Maintenance:** We'll explore how AI is used for predictive maintenance in mainframes, aiding in the early detection of potential issues and thereby reducing downtime.
- **ML for Data Analysis and Anomaly Detection:** The application of ML in analyzing large volumes of data and detecting anomalies will be examined. This is particularly relevant in ensuring the security and efficiency of mainframe operations.
- **Automated Decision Making:** The role of AI and ML in facilitating automated decision-making based on data insights will also be highlighted.

4.3. The Role of Cloud Computing in Mainframe Environments

Cloud computing has a significant role in modernizing mainframes, offering scalability, flexibility, and enhanced processing power. This section will cover how cloud technologies are being integrated with mainframes.

- **Hybrid Cloud Environments:** The concept of hybrid cloud environments, which combine the robustness of mainframes with the agility of cloud computing, will be explored.
- **Cloud-Based Automation Tools:** We will look at how cloud-based automation tools are being used to enhance the capabilities of mainframe systems.
- **Benefits of Cloud Integration:** The benefits, such as increased scalability, improved disaster recovery options, and enhanced data analytics capabilities, will be discussed.

Conclusion

This chapter will not only provide a detailed look into the tools and technologies driving modern automation but will also illustrate how they are being practically applied to enhance and transform mainframe environments.

4.1. Overview of Automation Tools

In the dynamic world of modern automation, a variety of tools play pivotal roles. This section provides a comprehensive overview of these tools, ranging from basic task automation to sophisticated platforms integrating AI, ML, and data analytics.

Task Automation Tools

- **Function and Application:** Task automation tools are designed to handle routine, repetitive tasks that are essential but time-consuming. This includes activities like data entry, batch processing, and routine system monitoring. These tools work by following predefined rules and scripts to execute tasks reliably and consistently.
- **Benefits:** The primary benefit of these tools is the significant time and resource savings they afford. By automating mundane tasks, they free up human resources for more complex and strategic activities.

Robotic Process Automation (RPA)

- **Replicating Human Actions:** RPA tools are at the forefront of modern automation. They are designed to replicate human interactions with software and systems, automating tasks like filling forms, extracting data, and processing transactions.

- **Non-Invasive Nature:** RPA is non-invasive and interacts with systems at the interface level, which means it can be implemented without altering existing systems. This makes RPA particularly attractive for automating tasks in legacy systems.
- **Use Cases:** Common use cases of RPA in business include automating data entry tasks, processing invoices, and managing customer queries, all of which significantly enhance operational efficiency.

Workflow Automation Platforms

- **Streamlining Business Processes:** Workflow automation platforms are crucial for automating and optimizing complex business processes. They help in designing, executing, and automating workflows that involve multiple steps and decision points.
- **Customization and Integration:** These platforms often offer customization options and can integrate with various other tools and systems, making them versatile solutions for a wide range of business needs.
- **Impact on Efficiency:** By automating workflows, these platforms can significantly enhance efficiency, reduce errors, and ensure consistency in business operations.

API-Based Automation

- **System Integration:** APIs (Application Programming Interfaces) play a critical role in modern automation by allowing different software systems to communicate and work together seamlessly. API-based automation is about using these interfaces to connect and automate interactions between disparate systems.

- **Flexibility and Scalability:** API-based automation offers flexibility and scalability, enabling businesses to integrate new functionalities and systems without significant overhauls.
- **Broad Applications:** The use of APIs is prevalent in scenarios where data needs to be synchronized across different systems or when actions in one system need to trigger a response in another, such as in integrating CRM systems with email marketing software.

Conclusion

From task-specific tools to complex platforms that integrate AI and ML, the landscape of modern automation tools is diverse and robust. Understanding the capabilities and applications of these tools is crucial for businesses looking to optimize their operations and embrace digital transformation.

Task Automation Tools

In the realm of modern automation, task automation tools are fundamental in enhancing operational efficiency. These tools are tailored to automate routine and repetitive tasks that, while essential, are often time-consuming and prone to human error.

Function and Application

- **Handling Routine Tasks:** Task automation tools are adept at managing a variety of routine, repetitive tasks across different business sectors. Common applications include data entry, where they input data into systems automatically; batch processing, where they execute batches of jobs without human intervention; and system monitoring, where they keep track of system performance and alert personnel to potential issues.
- **Predefined Rules and Scripts:** These tools operate based on predefined rules and scripts. For instance, in data entry, they might follow a script to extract data from a specific source and input it into a designated system. In system monitoring, they might be programmed to alert administrators if system performance falls below certain thresholds.
- **Consistency and Reliability:** By following set rules and scripts, task automation tools ensure tasks are performed consistently and reliably. This reduces the likelihood of errors that can occur with manual processing.

Benefits

- **Time and Resource Savings:** One of the most significant benefits of task automation tools is the substantial time and resource savings they offer. By automating mundane tasks, these tools free up valuable human resources, allowing employees to focus on more complex and strategic tasks that require human insight and decision-making.

- **Increased Productivity and Efficiency:** Automating routine tasks leads to increased productivity and efficiency. Tasks are completed faster and with greater accuracy, leading to streamlined operations and reduced turnaround times.
- **Enhancing Employee Satisfaction:** By relieving staff from monotonous, repetitive tasks, these tools can also lead to increased job satisfaction. Employees can engage in more meaningful and rewarding work, which can improve morale and reduce turnover.

Conclusion

Task automation tools are an integral component of modern automation strategies. By efficiently handling routine tasks, they not only save time and resources but also contribute to the overall effectiveness and productivity of business operations. As these tools continue to evolve, they will play an increasingly critical role in supporting and enhancing complex business processes.

Robotic Process Automation (RPA)

Robotic Process Automation (RPA) represents a significant advancement in the field of automation, providing a powerful tool for businesses to enhance efficiency and accuracy in their operations.

Replicating Human Actions

- **Mimicking Human Interaction:** RPA tools are designed to replicate the way humans interact with software and systems. By mimicking these actions, RPA can automate a wide range of tasks that typically require manual input or intervention.
- **Applications:** Common applications of RPA include filling out forms, where the tool automatically inputs data into fields; extracting data, where it retrieves information from documents or databases; and processing transactions, where it completes routine transactional tasks without human assistance.

Non-Invasive Nature

- **Interface-Level Interaction:** One of the defining characteristics of RPA is its non-invasive nature. These tools operate at the interface level, meaning they interact with systems in the same way a human user would, but without the need for backend integrations or alterations to existing systems.
- **Legacy System Compatibility:** This feature makes RPA particularly suitable for use with legacy systems, where more invasive automation technologies might not be feasible due to system constraints or the risk of disruption. RPA can be layered on top of these existing systems to automate tasks without the need for extensive system

modifications.

Use Cases in Business

- **Data Entry Automation:** RPA is widely used to automate data entry tasks, reducing the time and potential for error associated with manual data input. This includes entering customer information into CRM systems, updating records, or inputting data into ERP systems.
- **Invoice Processing:** In finance, RPA is often applied to invoice processing, where it can automatically extract data from invoices, match them with purchase orders, and process payments, streamlining the accounts payable process.
- **Customer Service:** In customer service, RPA can manage routine customer queries by fetching information from databases or executing standard responses, thereby enhancing response times and service quality.

Conclusion

Robotic Process Automation has emerged as a key player in the field of modern automation, offering a versatile, efficient, and user-friendly solution for automating a wide range of business processes. Its ability to work with existing systems with minimal disruption makes it an attractive option for businesses looking to automate without overhauling their current IT infrastructure.

Workflow Automation Platforms

Workflow automation platforms are pivotal in transforming how businesses operate, enabling them to automate and optimize complex processes with multiple steps and decision points.

Streamlining Business Processes

- **Design and Execution of Workflows:** These platforms are specifically designed to automate workflows, which are sequences of tasks that need to be completed to achieve a specific outcome. They enable the design and execution of these workflows in a manner that streamlines operations, reduces manual intervention, and increases process transparency.
- **Handling Multi-Step Processes:** Workflow automation is particularly effective in multi-step processes that involve various decision points. These platforms can manage the flow of information and tasks between different stages and stakeholders, ensuring that each step is completed in the correct sequence and timeframe.
- **Examples:** Common examples include the automation of procurement processes, from requisition to purchase order creation and approval, and onboarding processes where multiple departments are involved in setting up new employees.

Customization and Integration

- **Tailored Solutions:** Most workflow automation platforms offer robust customization options, allowing businesses to tailor workflows to their specific needs. This includes customizing forms, decision logic, and integrating specific business rules.

- **Integration Capabilities:** A key strength of these platforms is their ability to integrate with other tools and systems, such as CRM systems, ERP software, and document management systems. This integration ensures that data flows seamlessly across different business functions, enhancing overall operational coherence.

Impact on Efficiency

- **Enhanced Operational Efficiency:** By automating workflows, these platforms significantly enhance operational efficiency. Tasks that once required days to complete manually can now be processed in a matter of hours or even minutes.
- **Reduction in Errors:** Automation minimizes the risk of human error, which is particularly important in complex processes where a mistake at one stage can have cascading effects.
- **Consistency in Operations:** Workflow automation ensures a consistent approach to processes, which is crucial for maintaining quality and compliance standards. It provides a standardized method of handling tasks, ensuring that all process instances are executed in the same way.

Conclusion

Workflow automation platforms are an integral part of modern business operations, providing a powerful tool for streamlining complex processes, enhancing efficiency, and ensuring consistency. Their ability to be customized and integrated with other systems makes them a versatile solution suitable for a wide range of business needs.

API-Based Automation

API-based automation has become a cornerstone in the realm of modern automation, playing a pivotal role in enabling different software systems to interconnect and function cohesively.

System Integration

- **Role of APIs:** APIs (Application Programming Interfaces) are instrumental in modern automation, acting as the 'glue' that binds different software systems together. They allow these systems to communicate with each other, sharing data and functionalities seamlessly.
- **Automating Interactions:** API-based automation involves using these interfaces to automate the interactions between disparate systems. This can range from simple data transfers to more complex sequences of actions across multiple platforms.
- **Cross-System Workflow Automation:** APIs are particularly useful in automating workflows that span multiple systems. For example, an API can be used to automatically transfer customer data from a CRM system to a marketing platform, streamlining cross-departmental workflows.

Flexibility and Scalability

- **Adaptability to Business Needs:** One of the key advantages of API-based automation is its flexibility. APIs allow businesses to add new functionalities and integrate new systems without needing to overhaul their existing IT infrastructure.
- **Scalable Automation Solutions:** As a business grows and its needs evolve, API-based automation can scale accordingly. This scalability ensures that automation

strategies can adapt and grow in line with the business, providing a sustainable long-term solution.

Broad Applications

- **Versatile Usage:** The applications of API-based automation are extensive and diverse. They are widely used in scenarios where real-time data synchronization is crucial, such as syncing inventory data between an e-commerce platform and a warehouse management system.
- **Trigger-Based Actions:** APIs are also instrumental in scenarios where an action in one system needs to trigger a response in another. For instance, when a new lead is entered into a CRM system, an API can trigger a welcome email through an email marketing platform.
- **Enhancing Customer Experiences:** In customer service, APIs can automate the flow of customer interaction data across platforms, providing a more integrated and seamless customer experience.

Conclusion

API-based automation is a powerful tool in the modern automation toolkit, offering unparalleled flexibility, scalability, and breadth of application. Its ability to seamlessly integrate disparate systems makes it a critical component in creating efficient, responsive, and interconnected business processes.

4.2. Leveraging AI and Machine Learning in Mainframe Automation

Artificial Intelligence (AI) and Machine Learning (ML) are reshaping the landscape of mainframe automation, bringing a new level of intelligence and efficiency to these critical systems.

AI in Predictive Maintenance

- **Proactive System Management:** AI is revolutionizing the way mainframe maintenance is conducted. Through predictive maintenance, AI algorithms analyze patterns in system data to predict and preemptively address potential issues before they lead to system failure or downtime.
- **Reducing Downtime:** By identifying irregularities and potential faults early, AI-driven predictive maintenance can significantly reduce downtime and the associated costs. This proactive approach is far more efficient compared to traditional reactive maintenance models.
- **Example Applications:** Use cases include monitoring system performance metrics to predict hardware failures, or analyzing application performance data to identify areas that may need optimization or updates.

ML for Data Analysis and Anomaly Detection

- **Handling Vast Data Volumes:** ML algorithms are adept at analyzing large volumes of data generated by mainframe operations. This capability is critical in mainframes, where the sheer volume of data can be overwhelming for traditional analysis methods.
- **Anomaly Detection:** ML is particularly effective in anomaly detection. By learning what constitutes normal operation, ML algorithms can identify deviations that may indicate security breaches, system malfunctions, or other critical issues.
- **Enhancing Security and Efficiency:** The application of ML in anomaly detection plays a crucial role in enhancing both the security and efficiency of mainframe operations. It ensures that any unusual activity is quickly identified and addressed.

Automated Decision Making

- **Data-Driven Decisions:** AI and ML are not just about data analysis; they also facilitate automated decision-making. By processing and interpreting vast amounts of data, these technologies can make informed decisions much faster than human operators.
- **Improving Operational Efficiency:** Automated decision-making can significantly improve operational efficiency. Decisions based on real-time data and predictive analytics can optimize system performance, resource allocation, and overall mainframe management.
- **Applications:** This includes everything from automatically adjusting system resources based on workload demands, to

making real-time security decisions in the face of potential threats.

Conclusion

The integration of AI and ML into mainframe automation represents a significant leap forward in how these systems are managed and maintained. These technologies not only improve efficiency and reduce downtime but also enable a more proactive and data-driven approach to mainframe operations.

AI in Predictive Maintenance

The integration of Artificial Intelligence (AI) in predictive maintenance is transforming the approach to mainframe management, moving from reactive to proactive strategies.

Proactive System Management

- **Revolutionizing Maintenance Approaches:** AI algorithms are being utilized to revolutionize mainframe maintenance. Instead of reacting to problems as they occur, AI enables a proactive approach by analyzing data patterns and predicting potential issues.
- **Analyzing System Data:** AI algorithms scrutinize vast amounts of system data, identifying trends and patterns that might not be immediately apparent to human operators. This analysis includes everything from workload patterns to component performance.
- **Preemptive Issue Resolution:** By predicting issues before they manifest, AI-driven predictive maintenance allows for preemptive actions to be taken, thereby preventing system failures or significant downtime.

Reducing Downtime

- **Early Detection of Irregularities:** AI's ability to detect irregularities and potential faults early is crucial in minimizing downtime. By addressing issues before they escalate, AI helps maintain continuous system operation, which is critical for businesses relying on mainframe technology.
- **Cost-Efficiency:** This proactive approach not only reduces downtime but also lowers the associated costs. Preventive actions are typically less resource-intensive compared to

fixing major breakdowns, making AI a cost-efficient solution in system maintenance.

Example Applications

- **Predicting Hardware Failures:** AI algorithms can monitor hardware performance metrics, predicting failures before they occur. For example, they can detect signs of wear in disk drives or memory failures, prompting timely replacements or repairs.
- **Optimizing Application Performance:** In the realm of software, AI can analyze application performance data to identify inefficiencies or areas in need of optimization. This might involve flagging memory leaks or inefficient code that could hinder system performance.
- **Dynamic Resource Allocation:** AI can also be used to dynamically allocate resources based on predictive analysis. For instance, if an AI system predicts a spike in transaction processing, it can preemptively allocate additional resources to handle the increased load.

Conclusion

AI in predictive maintenance represents a forward-thinking approach to mainframe management, emphasizing prevention over reaction. This shift not only enhances the reliability and performance of mainframes but also offers significant cost savings and operational efficiencies.

ML for Data Analysis and Anomaly Detection

Machine Learning (ML) has become a pivotal technology in managing and analyzing the vast data volumes generated by mainframe operations. Its application, particularly in anomaly detection, is reshaping how mainframe security and operational efficiency are approached.

Handling Vast Data Volumes

- **Efficient Data Processing:** ML algorithms are exceptionally well-suited for sifting through and analyzing the large data sets produced by mainframes. Traditional data analysis methods often fall short in handling such volumes efficiently, but ML can process and analyze this data quickly and effectively.
- **Pattern Recognition:** ML excels in identifying patterns within large data sets. In mainframe environments, this ability is leveraged to understand normal operational patterns, making it easier to spot anomalies or irregularities that may indicate underlying issues.

Anomaly Detection

- **Learning Normal Operations:** A key strength of ML in anomaly detection is its ability to learn what constitutes normal operation for a particular mainframe system. By being trained on historical data, ML models develop an understanding of standard operational patterns and behaviors.
- **Identifying Deviations:** Once an ML model has learned the normal operational patterns, it can continuously monitor system data to identify deviations. These deviations, which might be subtle and not immediately

apparent to human observers, can indicate potential issues such as system malfunctions, security breaches, or performance bottlenecks.

Enhancing Security and Efficiency

- **Proactive Security Measures:** In terms of security, ML-driven anomaly detection is a game-changer. It enables proactive identification and mitigation of potential security threats, well before they can cause significant damage. This includes everything from detecting unusual access patterns that might signify a security breach to identifying potential vulnerabilities.
- **Operational Efficiency:** The efficiency of mainframe operations is significantly enhanced by ML. By automating the data analysis and anomaly detection processes, ML frees up valuable resources and allows for quicker, more effective responses to potential issues.
- **Continuous Improvement:** ML models can be continuously updated and improved with new data, enhancing their accuracy and reliability over time. This means that the system's ability to detect anomalies and optimize operations improves as it processes more data.

Conclusion

The integration of ML for data analysis and anomaly detection is transforming mainframe operations, making them more secure and efficient. By leveraging ML's capabilities, businesses can ensure their mainframes are not only robust and reliable but also capable of adapting to new challenges and evolving threats.

Automated Decision Making

Automated decision-making, powered by AI and ML, represents a significant advancement in the realm of mainframe automation. This technology not only analyzes data but also makes informed decisions autonomously, enhancing both efficiency and effectiveness in various operational aspects.

Data-Driven Decisions

- **Enhanced Decision-Making Process:** AI and ML transform the decision-making process by leveraging vast amounts of data. These technologies can analyze complex datasets much faster than human operators, leading to quicker and more informed decisions.
- **Accuracy and Speed:** The strength of AI and ML in decision-making lies in their ability to process and interpret large volumes of data with high accuracy and speed. This capability allows for decisions to be made based on comprehensive data analysis, reducing the likelihood of errors that can occur in human judgment.

Improving Operational Efficiency

- **Optimizing System Performance:** Automated decision-making plays a critical role in optimizing mainframe performance. By analyzing real-time data, AI and ML can make decisions that enhance system efficiency, such as allocating resources more effectively or adjusting operational parameters to optimize performance.
- **Predictive Analytics:** Utilizing predictive analytics, these systems can forecast future trends or potential issues, allowing for preemptive actions that prevent problems and maximize system uptime.

- **Resource Allocation:** In the context of mainframes, automated decision-making can dynamically allocate system resources based on current workload demands, ensuring optimal use of computational power and storage capacity.

Applications

- **Dynamic Resource Adjustment:** An application of automated decision-making in mainframes is the dynamic adjustment of system resources. For example, AI algorithms can analyze current workload and automatically allocate additional resources to handle high-demand periods, ensuring consistent performance without manual intervention.
- **Real-Time Security Decisions:** In the realm of security, AI-driven systems can monitor for potential threats and make real-time decisions to counteract them. This might include identifying and isolating suspicious activities or automatically updating security protocols in response to detected vulnerabilities.
- **Operational Automation:** Automated decision-making also finds applications in operational tasks such as data backup scheduling, system maintenance planning, and even in business-oriented decisions like pricing strategies or customer segmentation based on real-time data analysis.

Conclusion

The use of AI and ML for automated decision-making in mainframe environments marks a significant shift towards more autonomous, efficient, and effective system management. These technologies not only enhance operational efficiency but also open up new avenues for proactive system management and strategic business decision-making.

4.3. The Role of Cloud Computing in Mainframe Environments

Cloud computing is playing an increasingly crucial role in the modernization of mainframe environments. It offers a range of benefits, from enhanced scalability to improved disaster recovery options, fundamentally changing how mainframe resources are utilized and managed.

Hybrid Cloud Environments

- **Combining Mainframes and Cloud:** Hybrid cloud environments represent the integration of the traditional robustness of mainframe systems with the agility and flexibility of cloud computing. This approach allows businesses to leverage the strengths of both architectures.
- **Flexibility and Modernization:** Hybrid cloud environments enable mainframe users to access modern cloud services and infrastructures, such as scalable storage and advanced analytics platforms, while still maintaining the core processing power and reliability of their mainframe systems.
- **Seamless Integration:** The key to a successful hybrid

cloud environment is seamless integration, where data and applications can move fluidly between mainframe and cloud platforms. This requires sophisticated networking and security measures to ensure data integrity and compliance.

Cloud-Based Automation Tools

- **Enhancing Mainframe Capabilities:** Cloud-based automation tools are being increasingly used to augment the capabilities of mainframe systems. These tools can automate various tasks, including workload scheduling, system monitoring, and even some aspects of security management.
- **Accessibility and Innovation:** By leveraging cloud-based tools, mainframe environments can access a broader range of functionalities and innovative solutions that may not be available within the traditional mainframe ecosystem.

Benefits of Cloud Integration

- **Increased Scalability:** One of the primary benefits of integrating cloud computing with mainframes is increased scalability. Cloud environments can easily scale resources up or down based on demand, providing mainframe systems with a level of flexibility that is difficult to achieve otherwise.
- **Improved Disaster Recovery:** Cloud platforms offer robust disaster recovery options. By integrating mainframes with the cloud, businesses can ensure more efficient data backups, quicker recovery times, and improved data redundancy.

- **Enhanced Data Analytics Capabilities:** The cloud provides access to advanced data analytics tools and services. Integrating these tools with mainframe data allows businesses to gain deeper insights, supporting more informed decision-making processes.
- **Cost Efficiency:** Cloud integration can also lead to cost savings. The ability to leverage cloud resources means that businesses can optimize their mainframe utilization and reduce costs associated with data storage and processing.

Conclusion

The integration of cloud computing with mainframe environments represents a significant advancement in mainframe technology. It offers a pathway to modernization, providing mainframe users with enhanced flexibility, scalability, and access to advanced tools that were previously beyond their reach.

Hybrid Cloud Environments

Hybrid cloud environments are emerging as a transformative solution for mainframe users, blending the stability and power of mainframes with the agility and innovation of cloud computing. This combination offers a powerful approach to modernizing legacy systems.

Combining Mainframes and Cloud

- **Leveraging Dual Strengths:** Hybrid cloud environments are about leveraging the best of both worlds. The robustness, processing power, and security of traditional mainframe systems are combined with the scalability, flexibility, and modern functionalities of cloud computing.
- **Strategic Integration:** This approach is not about replacing mainframes but integrating them with cloud technologies. Businesses can thus continue to utilize their existing mainframe investments while also taking advantage of the modern features offered by cloud platforms.

Flexibility and Modernization

- **Access to Modern Services:** Mainframe users in a hybrid cloud environment have access to a range of modern cloud services and infrastructures. This includes scalable storage solutions, advanced data analytics platforms, and cutting-edge development tools.
- **Continuous Innovation:** Hybrid environments enable continuous innovation within mainframe systems. Mainframe users can integrate new technologies and services as they become available in the cloud, keeping the mainframe environment up-to-date and competitive.

Seamless Integration

- **Fluid Data and Application Movement:** A critical aspect of hybrid cloud environments is the seamless integration that allows for fluid movement of data and applications between the mainframe and cloud platforms. This integration is crucial for maintaining consistency and ensuring uninterrupted business operations.
- **Networking and Security:** Successful integration requires sophisticated networking solutions and robust security measures. Ensuring data integrity and compliance, especially in regulated industries, is paramount. This includes implementing secure data transmission channels, robust encryption protocols, and compliance with data privacy regulations.
- **Managing Complexity:** The integration process involves managing the inherent complexity of combining two fundamentally different architectures. It requires a deep understanding of both mainframe and cloud technologies and the development of a strategic approach to bridge these platforms effectively.

Conclusion

Hybrid cloud environments represent a strategic evolution in mainframe utilization, offering a path to modernization that capitalizes on existing mainframe investments while embracing the innovations of cloud technology. This approach provides businesses with the flexibility, scalability, and modern capabilities necessary to thrive in today's rapidly evolving technological landscape.

Cloud-Based Automation Tools

The integration of cloud-based automation tools with mainframe systems represents a significant step in modernizing and enhancing the capabilities of these traditionally robust systems. These tools bring a new dimension of efficiency, flexibility, and innovation to mainframe operations.

Enhancing Mainframe Capabilities

- **Automating Routine Tasks:** Cloud-based automation tools can handle a variety of tasks that are essential yet time-consuming for mainframe operations. This includes automating workload scheduling, ensuring that tasks are processed efficiently and resources are optimally utilized.
- **Advanced System Monitoring:** System monitoring, a critical aspect of mainframe management, can be significantly enhanced by cloud-based tools. These tools can provide more comprehensive monitoring capabilities, offering real-time insights and predictive analytics for system performance and health.
- **Security Management:** Some cloud-based automation tools also extend their functionalities to security management. They can automate routine security checks, update security protocols, and even identify potential vulnerabilities, thereby enhancing the overall security posture of mainframe systems.

Accessibility and Innovation

- **Broadening Functional Range:** One of the key advantages of incorporating cloud-based tools into mainframe environments is the access they provide to a wider range of functionalities. This includes advanced analytics, AI-driven insights, and innovative management solutions that might not be native to traditional mainframe systems.

- **Continuous Access to New Technologies:** Cloud platforms are continually evolving, with new tools and features being regularly introduced. By integrating with cloud-based automation tools, mainframe environments can benefit from these advancements, continually modernizing and improving their operations.
- **Customizable Solutions:** Many cloud-based automation tools offer a high degree of customization. This means that mainframe operators can tailor these tools to fit their specific needs, ensuring that the automation aligns perfectly with their operational requirements.

Conclusion

Cloud-based automation tools offer a pathway to significantly enhance the capabilities of mainframe systems. By adopting these tools, mainframes can not only maintain their inherent strengths but also embrace new technologies and innovations, driving efficiency, security, and operational excellence.

Benefits of Cloud Integration

Integrating cloud computing with mainframes brings a host of benefits, enhancing scalability, disaster recovery, data analytics, and cost efficiency. This integration represents a significant step forward in the evolution of mainframe computing.

Increased Scalability

- **Dynamic Resource Allocation:** Cloud environments excel in scalability, allowing resources to be scaled up or down based on demand. This flexibility is particularly beneficial for mainframe systems, traditionally known for their fixed resource capacity.
- **Handling Variable Workloads:** The integration with cloud computing enables mainframe systems to handle variable workloads more efficiently. During peak periods, additional cloud resources can be utilized to manage the load, ensuring consistent performance without the need for physical hardware expansion.

Improved Disaster Recovery

- **Robust Backup Solutions:** Cloud platforms provide robust options for disaster recovery. By integrating mainframes with the cloud, businesses can implement more efficient and reliable data backup solutions.
- **Quick Recovery Times:** Cloud-based disaster recovery strategies often offer quicker recovery times compared to traditional methods. This rapid recovery capability is crucial for maintaining business continuity in the event of system failures or other disruptions.
- **Data Redundancy:** The cloud offers improved data redundancy, storing data across multiple locations. This

geographical distribution of data enhances its safety and ensures that critical data is not lost in case of local failures.

Enhanced Data Analytics Capabilities

- **Access to Advanced Tools:** Cloud integration opens up access to advanced data analytics tools and services that might not be natively available in mainframe environments. These tools can process and analyze large volumes of data, providing valuable insights.
- **Supporting Informed Decision-Making:** By leveraging cloud-based analytics with mainframe data, businesses can gain deeper insights into their operations. This supports more informed and data-driven decision-making processes, enhancing strategic planning and operational efficiency.

Cost Efficiency

- **Optimizing Resource Utilization:** Cloud integration allows businesses to use mainframe resources more optimally. By leveraging cloud resources for additional capacity or specific functionalities, businesses can avoid the costs associated with physical infrastructure expansion.
- **Reducing Storage and Processing Costs:** The cloud's pay-as-you-go model offers cost savings in terms of data storage and processing. Businesses only pay for the cloud resources they use, providing a cost-effective solution for scaling and managing IT operations.

Conclusion

The integration of cloud computing with mainframe systems offers significant benefits, transforming how businesses manage and utilize these powerful systems. From scalability and disaster recovery to enhanced analytics and cost efficiency, cloud integration represents a strategic advantage in the modernization of mainframe environments.

Chapter 5. Integrating Automation with Mainframe Operations

Integrating automation within mainframe operations is a strategic process that requires careful planning, adherence to best practices, and effective management of change and user adoption. This chapter explores these critical components to ensure a successful integration of automation technologies in mainframe environments.

5.1. Planning and Strategy for Automation Integration

- **Assessment of Current Systems:** The first step involves a thorough assessment of the existing mainframe environment to identify areas that can benefit most from automation. This includes understanding current workflows, system capabilities, and potential limitations.
- **Defining Objectives:** Clear objectives for automation integration should be set, aligning with the overall business goals. This might include improving system efficiency, reducing operational costs, or enhancing service quality.
- **Developing a Roadmap:** A strategic roadmap for integration should be developed, outlining key milestones, timelines, and required resources. This roadmap should consider both the technical aspects of integration and the

business impacts.

- **Risk Management:** Identifying potential risks and developing mitigation strategies is crucial. This includes technical risks, such as system compatibility issues, as well as operational risks, like potential disruptions during the integration process.

5.2. Best Practices in Automation Deployment

- **Iterative Approach:** Adopting an iterative approach to automation deployment allows for gradual implementation and fine-tuning. This can help in minimizing disruptions and ensuring system stability.
- **Testing and Validation:** Rigorous testing of automation solutions before full-scale deployment is essential. This should include testing for functionality, performance, and security.
- **Documentation and Training:** Comprehensive documentation of the automation processes and adequate training for staff are vital. This ensures that team members are well-equipped to handle the new automated systems.
- **Monitoring and Continuous Improvement:** Continuous monitoring of the automated systems post-deployment is necessary to ensure they are functioning as intended. Regular reviews should be conducted to identify opportunities for further improvements.

5.3. Managing Change and User Adoption

- **Effective Communication:** Clear and consistent communication about the automation integration, its benefits, and its impacts on various roles is important for managing change.

- **User Involvement:** Involving users in the planning and implementation phases can aid in easing the transition. User feedback should be encouraged and used to refine the automation processes.
- **Support Structures:** Establishing support structures, such as help desks or user groups, can assist staff in adapting to the new automated environment.
- **Cultural Shift:** Encouraging a cultural shift towards embracing automation and innovation can significantly improve user adoption. Leadership plays a key role in fostering this cultural change.

Conclusion

Integrating automation with mainframe operations is a multifaceted process that requires strategic planning, adherence to best practices, and effective management of change. A well-executed integration can significantly enhance the efficiency, reliability, and scalability of mainframe operations.

5.1. Planning and Strategy for Automation Integration

Integrating automation into mainframe operations is a complex process that requires careful planning and strategy. A well-thought-out approach ensures that automation not only aligns with business goals but also enhances the existing mainframe environment.

Assessment of Current Systems

- **Understanding the Environment:** A comprehensive assessment of the current mainframe environment is essential. This involves evaluating existing workflows, understanding the capabilities of the current system, and identifying any limitations or bottlenecks that could impact automation.
- **Identifying Automation Opportunities:** This stage also includes identifying areas where automation can bring the most benefit. This could be in processes that are highly repetitive, prone to error, or particularly time-consuming.
- **Technical Evaluation:** A technical evaluation should be conducted to understand the compatibility of new automation tools with the existing mainframe system. This

includes hardware, software, and network assessments.

Defining Objectives

- **Aligning with Business Goals:** The objectives for automation integration should closely align with the broader business goals. Clear, well-defined objectives guide the entire integration process and ensure that the automation efforts are focused and effective.
- **Examples of Objectives:** Objectives may include improving the efficiency of system operations, reducing the time and cost of specific processes, enhancing the accuracy of operations, or improving service delivery.

Developing a Roadmap

- **Strategic Planning:** Developing a strategic roadmap for automation integration is crucial. This roadmap should outline the key milestones, timelines for implementation, and the resources required.
- **Balancing Technical and Business Needs:** The roadmap should balance both technical and business considerations. It must address the technical aspects of integrating new tools while also considering the impact on business operations, employee roles, and service delivery.

Risk Management

- **Identifying Potential Risks:** A thorough risk assessment is essential to identify potential challenges that might arise during the integration process. This includes both technical risks, like system incompatibilities, and operational risks, such as potential disruptions to business processes.

- **Mitigation Strategies:** Developing strategies to mitigate these risks is a critical part of the planning process. This might involve phased implementation, additional staff training, or establishing backup processes.

Conclusion

Effective planning and strategic development are foundational to successfully integrating automation into mainframe operations. This process requires a careful assessment of the current system, clear objective setting, a well-defined roadmap, and comprehensive risk management strategies.

Assessment of Current Systems

The first step in integrating automation into mainframe operations is a comprehensive assessment of the current systems. This assessment lays the groundwork for a successful automation strategy by identifying key areas for improvement and potential challenges.

Understanding the Environment

- **Evaluating Workflows:** It's crucial to start with an in-depth evaluation of the existing workflows within the mainframe environment. Understanding how various processes are currently handled helps in identifying inefficiencies or manual processes that could be automated.
- **System Capabilities:** Assessing the capabilities of the current system includes examining the processing power, memory, storage, and overall system architecture. This helps in understanding how well the system can support additional automation tools or processes.
- **Limitations and Bottlenecks:** Identifying any existing limitations or bottlenecks is essential. This could involve areas where the system is underperforming, processes that are particularly slow or error-prone, or where data congestion occurs.

Identifying Automation Opportunities

- **Targeting Repetitive and Time-Consuming Processes:** Focus should be on identifying processes that are highly repetitive, prone to human error, or time-consuming. These are typically the areas where automation can have the most significant impact.
- **Evaluating for Error Reduction:** Processes that have a high rate of error due to manual intervention are prime

candidates for automation. Automating these processes can improve accuracy and consistency.

- **Assessing for Efficiency Gains:** Processes that are essential but do not necessarily add direct value (e.g., data entry, report generation) are also good candidates for automation, as automating these can free up valuable resources for more strategic tasks.

Technical Evaluation

- **Compatibility with Automation Tools:** A technical evaluation of the existing mainframe system is necessary to determine the compatibility with new automation tools. This involves assessing the hardware and software to ensure they can support the proposed automation solutions.
- **Network Assessment:** Evaluating the network infrastructure is also crucial, especially in terms of bandwidth and security. This ensures that the network can handle increased loads and data transfers associated with automated processes.
- **Integration Capabilities:** Understanding the integration capabilities of the existing system with potential automation tools is key. This includes assessing APIs, data exchange formats, and interoperability with cloud-based or other external systems.

Conclusion

A thorough assessment of the current mainframe systems is a critical step in the automation integration process. It helps in identifying the best opportunities for automation, understanding system capabilities and limitations, and ensuring compatibility with new technologies.

Defining Objectives

Setting clear and strategic objectives is a crucial step in the process of integrating automation with mainframe operations. These objectives should be in harmony with the broader goals of the business and serve as a guiding force for the entire integration process.

Aligning with Business Goals

- **Understanding Business Priorities:** The first step in defining objectives is to have a deep understanding of the business's overarching goals and priorities. This understanding ensures that the automation efforts are not just technologically sound but also bring real business value.
- **Strategic Alignment:** The objectives for automation should be strategically aligned with key business goals, whether they are related to growth, efficiency, innovation, customer satisfaction, or cost reduction.
- **Stakeholder Engagement:** Engaging with stakeholders from different business units can provide valuable insights into how automation can best support the business. This includes discussions with IT teams, operations managers, and executive leadership.

Examples of Objectives

- **Improving System Efficiency:** An objective could be to improve the overall efficiency of mainframe operations. This might involve automating routine tasks, optimizing system workflows, or enhancing resource allocation.
- **Reducing Process Time and Cost:** Another common objective is the reduction of time and cost for specific

processes. Automation can streamline processes that are currently labor-intensive and time-consuming, leading to significant cost savings.

- **Enhancing Operational Accuracy:** Improving the accuracy of operations is a critical objective, especially in environments where errors can have significant consequences. Automation can reduce the likelihood of human error in tasks such as data entry, calculations, and reporting.
- **Improving Service Delivery:** For businesses where mainframes play a role in customer service, an objective might be to use automation to enhance service delivery. This could include faster processing of customer requests or more personalized service through data analysis.

Conclusion

Defining clear objectives for the integration of automation in mainframe operations is pivotal. These objectives ensure that the automation efforts are not only technically successful but also deliver tangible business benefits, aligning with and supporting the overall goals of the organization.

Developing a Roadmap

Creating a strategic roadmap for the integration of automation into mainframe operations is an essential step. This roadmap serves as a blueprint, guiding the implementation process and ensuring that all aspects of the integration are carefully planned and executed.

Strategic Planning

- **Outlining Key Milestones:** The roadmap should clearly outline key milestones in the integration process. This includes the initial assessment phase, selection of automation tools, pilot testing, full-scale implementation, and post-implementation review.
- **Setting Realistic Timelines:** Establishing realistic timelines for each phase of the integration is crucial. These timelines should consider the complexity of the tasks, the availability of resources, and potential challenges that might arise.
- **Resource Allocation:** Identifying and allocating the necessary resources for each phase of the integration is essential. This includes budgeting for new software and hardware, as well as allocating human resources such as IT staff and external consultants.

Balancing Technical and Business Needs

- **Technical Integration:** The roadmap must address the technical aspects of integrating new automation tools with the existing mainframe system. This involves considerations around system compatibility, data migration, and integration with existing workflows.
- **Business Impact:** Equally important is the consideration of the integration's impact on business operations. The

roadmap should address how automation will affect existing business processes, employee roles, and overall service delivery.

- **Change Management:** Integrating new technologies often requires changes in business processes and employee responsibilities. The roadmap should therefore include strategies for managing these changes, including training programs, communication plans, and support systems.
- **Continuous Evaluation:** Throughout the integration process, continuous evaluation should be conducted to ensure that the project is aligned with the roadmap. Adjustments may be necessary based on feedback and the results of each phase.

Conclusion

A well-crafted roadmap is essential for the successful integration of automation into mainframe operations. It provides a structured approach to the integration, ensuring that both technical and business needs are met and that the project is completed on time and within budget.

Risk Management

Effective risk management is a critical component of integrating automation into mainframe operations. It involves identifying potential risks and developing strategies to mitigate them, ensuring a smooth and successful integration process.

Identifying Potential Risks

- **Technical Risks:** These include risks associated with system incompatibilities, data migration challenges, or issues related to software or hardware integration. Identifying these risks requires a deep understanding of both the existing mainframe system and the new automation technologies.
- **Operational Risks:** Operational risks might include potential disruptions to business processes during the integration phase, impacts on service delivery, or challenges in adapting to new workflows. Understanding the operational flow and how automation will impact it is crucial in identifying these risks.
- **Human Factors:** Risks related to human factors, such as resistance to change or skill gaps in handling new systems, should also be assessed. These risks can significantly impact the adoption and effectiveness of the automation integration.

Mitigation Strategies

- **Phased Implementation:** Implementing automation in phases can help mitigate risks by allowing for adjustments based on feedback at each stage. This approach enables issues to be identified and resolved early, reducing the impact on the overall project.

- **Staff Training and Support:** Providing comprehensive training and support to staff is vital to manage the risk associated with human factors. This includes not only technical training but also education on the benefits and changes brought by automation.
- **Backup Processes:** Establishing backup processes and contingency plans is crucial to mitigate operational risks. This ensures that business operations can continue smoothly in case of any disruptions during the integration process.
- **Testing and Validation:** Rigorous testing and validation of the automation integration at each stage can help identify and address technical risks before they escalate. This includes testing for compatibility, performance, and security.

Conclusion

Risk management in the integration of automation into mainframe operations involves a careful assessment of potential risks and the development of targeted strategies to address them. By proactively managing these risks, businesses can ensure a smoother transition to automated systems and minimize the impact on operations.

5.2. Best Practices in Automation Deployment

The deployment of automation in mainframe environments should adhere to a set of best practices to ensure successful implementation and long-term sustainability. These practices are designed to minimize risks, enhance system performance, and ensure that staff are well-prepared to adapt to new automated processes.

Iterative Approach

- **Gradual Implementation:** An iterative approach allows for a gradual rollout of automation solutions. This method helps in identifying potential issues early in the process, allowing for adjustments before a full-scale deployment.
- **Fine-Tuning Systems:** By deploying automation in stages, organizations can fine-tune systems based on initial feedback and performance metrics. This iterative refinement ensures a more stable and effective automation system.
- **Minimizing Disruptions:** Gradual implementation helps in minimizing disruptions to existing operations, as staff and systems can adjust to changes in a controlled manner.

Testing and Validation

- **Functionality Testing:** Before deploying an automation solution, it is crucial to rigorously test its functionality to ensure it meets the required specifications and integrates well with existing systems.
- **Performance Evaluation:** Testing should also assess the performance of the automation solution under various scenarios to ensure it can handle expected workloads and processes efficiently.
- **Security Assessment:** Given the critical nature of mainframe systems, thorough security testing is essential to safeguard against vulnerabilities that could be introduced by the new automation tools.

Documentation and Training

- **Clear Documentation:** Comprehensive documentation of the automation processes, including operational guidelines and troubleshooting steps, is essential. This serves as a reference for the team and assists in resolving issues that may arise.
- **Staff Training:** Equipping staff with the necessary training to handle new automated systems is vital. Training should cover both the technical aspects of the automation tools and the operational changes they bring about.

Monitoring and Continuous Improvement

- **Ongoing Monitoring:** Continuous monitoring of the automated systems post-deployment is crucial to ensure they function as intended. This includes monitoring system performance, user interactions, and overall system health.

- **Regular Reviews for Improvements:** Regularly reviewing the performance of the automation system allows for the identification of areas for improvement. This continuous improvement cycle ensures the system remains efficient and relevant.

Conclusion

Following these best practices in automation deployment is key to achieving a successful integration of automation technologies in mainframe environments. It ensures a smooth transition, minimizes risks, and fosters an environment of continuous improvement.

Iterative Approach

Adopting an iterative approach to the deployment of automation solutions in mainframe environments is essential for ensuring a smooth transition and effective system performance. This approach . facilitates gradual implementation, allowing for continuous assessment and refinement.

Gradual Implementation

- **Phased Rollout:** Implementing automation solutions gradually, in phases, allows organizations to manage the transition effectively. Each phase can focus on a specific area or process, making it easier to track and evaluate the impact of automation.
- **Early Issue Identification:** A gradual rollout helps in early identification of potential issues or challenges. Detecting and addressing these issues in the early stages of deployment can prevent them from becoming more significant problems during a full-scale implementation.
- **Feedback Integration:** This approach also allows for the incorporation of feedback from users and stakeholders at each stage, ensuring that the automation solutions are aligned with user needs and business objectives.

Fine-Tuning Systems

- **Continuous Refinement:** After each phase of the rollout, the automation system can be reviewed and refined based on performance metrics and user feedback. This fine-tuning process ensures that the system is optimized for efficiency and effectiveness.
- **Performance Optimization:** By analyzing the performance data from each phase, organizations can make

informed decisions about how to adjust and improve the system for better results.

Minimizing Disruptions

- **Controlled Adjustments:** A gradual implementation minimizes disruptions to existing operations. As the automation is rolled out in stages, staff and other systems have time to adjust to the changes, reducing the impact on daily operations.
- **Training and Adaptation:** This phased approach provides ample opportunity for staff training and adaptation. Employees can become familiar with the new system gradually, which can ease the transition and reduce resistance to change.
- **Risk Mitigation:** By implementing automation solutions iteratively, organizations can mitigate the risk of major disruptions or system failures, as any issues are likely to be less extensive and easier to resolve.

Conclusion

An iterative approach to deploying automation solutions in mainframe environments is a strategic method that allows for gradual implementation, system fine-tuning, and minimization of operational disruptions. This approach not only facilitates smoother integration but also ensures that the automation system is optimized for performance and aligned with business needs.

Testing and Validation

Testing and validation are critical stages in the deployment of automation solutions in mainframe environments. This process ensures that the automation not only functions as intended but also maintains the integrity and security of the mainframe system.

Functionality Testing

- **Conformance to Specifications:** Functionality testing involves verifying that the automation solution meets all specified requirements. This includes ensuring that the solution performs the desired tasks accurately and integrates seamlessly with existing mainframe applications and workflows.
- **Integration Testing:** Special attention should be paid to how the new automation solution integrates with existing systems. This includes testing interfaces, data exchange mechanisms, and workflow triggers to ensure smooth operation within the mainframe environment.
- **User Acceptance Testing (UAT):** UAT is crucial to confirm that the automation solution meets the needs and expectations of its end-users. This phase often involves real-world scenario testing by actual system users.

Performance Evaluation

- **Load Testing:** Performance evaluation involves testing the automation solution under various load conditions. Load testing helps determine how the system behaves under peak usage scenarios and whether it can handle the expected workload.
- **Stress Testing:** Stress testing is important to understand how the system performs under extreme conditions. This

helps identify the breaking point of the automation solution and areas that need reinforcement.

- **Response Time Measurements:** Assessing the response times of automated processes ensures that they meet the performance standards required for mainframe operations.

Security Assessment

- **Vulnerability Analysis:** Given the sensitive and critical nature of mainframe systems, conducting a thorough security assessment is imperative. This includes vulnerability analysis to identify any security weaknesses introduced by the automation solution.
- **Penetration Testing:** Penetration testing simulates attacks on the system to assess the security of the automation solution. This test helps identify any potential breaches or data leaks that could be exploited.
- **Compliance Checks:** Ensuring that the automation solution complies with relevant security standards and regulations is also crucial, especially for industries governed by strict data protection laws.

Conclusion

Rigorous testing and validation are indispensable in the successful deployment of automation solutions in mainframe environments. These steps ensure that the automation not only performs efficiently and effectively but also maintains the high levels of security and reliability expected of mainframe systems.

Documentation and Training

Successful integration of automation into mainframe operations requires not only technical implementation but also comprehensive documentation and effective staff training. These components are essential for ensuring that the team can effectively manage and utilize the new automated systems.

Clear Documentation

- **Creating a Reference Resource:** Documentation should serve as a detailed reference guide covering all aspects of the automation processes. This includes operational guidelines, system configurations, workflow descriptions, and user manuals.
- **Troubleshooting Guides:** Including troubleshooting steps and solutions to common issues in the documentation is crucial. This empowers the team to resolve problems quickly and efficiently, minimizing downtime.
- **Version Control and Updates:** Documentation should be kept up-to-date, especially when system updates or changes are made. Implementing version control for documentation ensures that all team members have access to the latest information.
- **Accessible Formats:** Documentation should be made available in accessible formats and stored in a central, easily accessible location. This could be a digital knowledge base or a physical repository, depending on the organization's preference.

Staff Training

- **Technical Skill Development:** Training should focus on developing the technical skills necessary for operating the new automation tools. This includes understanding the software interface, managing automated workflows, and monitoring system performance.

- **Understanding Operational Changes:** Staff should also be trained on how the automation affects their day-to-day operations. This includes understanding new workflows, changes in job roles, and how to interact with the automated system.
- **Customized Training Programs:** Training programs should be tailored to the specific needs of different user groups within the organization. For example, IT staff may require more in-depth technical training, while end-users might need more focus on operational aspects.
- **Continuous Learning and Support:** Post-training support should be provided to ensure staff can effectively apply their new skills. This could include regular follow-up sessions, Q&A forums, or access to additional learning resources.

Conclusion

Effective documentation and training are critical to the successful integration of automation in mainframe operations. They ensure that the team is well-prepared to handle the new systems and that they have the resources needed to manage and troubleshoot the automated processes effectively.

Monitoring and Continuous Improvement

After deploying automation in mainframe operations, ongoing monitoring and continuous improvement are essential to maintain system efficiency and effectiveness. These practices ensure that the automated systems consistently meet performance standards and adapt to evolving business needs.

Ongoing Monitoring

- **System Performance Monitoring:** Continuous monitoring involves regularly checking the performance of the automated systems. Key performance indicators (KPIs) should be established to measure efficiency, speed, accuracy, and reliability.
- **User Interactions Tracking:** Monitoring how users interact with the automated systems can provide insights into usability and identify areas where additional training or system adjustments may be needed.
- **Health Checks:** Regular system health checks are essential to ensure all components of the automated system are functioning optimally. This includes monitoring for potential technical issues like system overloads, memory leaks, or network bottlenecks.
- **Alert Systems:** Implementing automated alerts for any anomalies or system failures can help in quickly identifying and addressing issues, minimizing potential impacts on operations.

Regular Reviews for Improvements

- **Performance Analysis:** Regular reviews of the system's performance against the established KPIs can help in identifying trends, successes, and areas for improvement.

This analysis should consider both quantitative data (like processing times and error rates) and qualitative feedback from users.

- **Iterative Refinements:** Based on the performance analysis, iterative refinements should be made to the automation system. This could involve optimizing workflows, updating software, or reconfiguring hardware components.
- **Adaptation to Changing Needs:** As business needs evolve, the automation system may need to adapt. Regular reviews provide an opportunity to align the system with changing requirements, ensuring continued relevance and effectiveness.
- **Stakeholder Feedback:** Incorporating feedback from stakeholders, including IT staff, end-users, and management, is crucial in the continuous improvement process. This feedback can provide diverse perspectives on how the automation system is performing and areas where it can be enhanced.

Conclusion

Ongoing monitoring and continuous improvement are crucial for maximizing the benefits of automation in mainframe operations. These practices ensure that automated systems not only meet current operational requirements but are also adaptable to future changes and advancements.

5.3. Managing Change and User Adoption

Successfully integrating automation into mainframe operations involves more than just the technical deployment; it requires effective management of change and fostering user adoption. This process is critical for ensuring that the transition is smooth and that the new automated systems are embraced and effectively utilized.

Effective Communication

- **Clarity on Automation Goals:** Communication should clearly articulate the purpose and goals of the automation integration. Understanding why changes are being made helps build a positive perspective among users.
- **Benefits and Impacts:** It's important to communicate the benefits of automation, such as increased efficiency and reduced manual workload, as well as how it might impact various roles within the organization.
- **Ongoing Dialogue:** Establishing channels for ongoing communication throughout the integration process helps in addressing concerns, sharing updates, and maintaining transparency.

User Involvement

- **Participation in Planning:** Involving users in the planning stages of automation projects helps in ensuring that the system meets actual work requirements and user needs.
- **Feedback Mechanisms:** Implementing mechanisms for collecting and incorporating user feedback into the automation process is crucial. This feedback can be invaluable in refining and improving the system.
- **User-Centric Design:** Designing the automated processes with the end-user in mind enhances usability and acceptance. User involvement in this design process can lead to more intuitive and user-friendly systems.

Support Structures

- **Help Desks and Support Teams:** Establishing dedicated support structures, such as help desks or technical support teams, can provide users with the assistance they need as they adapt to the new system.
- **Training and Resource Centers:** Providing access to training materials, user guides, and resource centers helps users become more comfortable and proficient with the automated systems.

Cultural Shift

- **Promoting a Culture of Innovation:** Leadership should actively promote a culture that embraces automation and innovation. This includes recognizing and rewarding adaptability, innovation, and continuous learning.
- **Change Champions:** Identifying and empowering change champions within the organization can help in driving the cultural shift. These individuals can advocate for the

benefits of automation and assist their colleagues in navigating the changes.

- **Addressing Resistance:** Understanding and addressing resistance to change is important. This may involve addressing fears about job security or the belief that automation may not be as effective as existing processes.

Conclusion

Managing change and user adoption is a pivotal aspect of integrating automation into mainframe operations. Effective communication, user involvement, support structures, and fostering a cultural shift are key strategies to ensure that the integration is not only technically successful but also well-received and utilized by the workforce.

Effective Communication

Effective communication is a cornerstone in managing the integration of automation into mainframe operations. It plays a vital role in ensuring that all stakeholders understand, accept, and support the transition.

Clarity on Automation Goals

- **Articulating the Purpose:** Clear communication about the objectives and purpose of the automation integration is essential. This involves explaining the rationale behind the decision to automate, the expected outcomes, and how it aligns with the broader organizational goals.
- **Setting Expectations:** It's important to set realistic expectations regarding the automation project. This includes discussing timelines, potential challenges, and the anticipated benefits once the system is fully integrated.

Benefits and Impacts

- **Highlighting Advantages:** Regularly communicating the benefits of automation is key. This can include improved operational efficiency, accuracy, and the potential for more engaging and strategic work for employees as routine tasks become automated.
- **Addressing Role Changes:** Communication should also address how automation will impact different roles within the organization. Being transparent about changes in job responsibilities and how employees can transition into new roles or responsibilities is crucial.
- **Reassuring Job Security:** Addressing concerns about job displacement upfront is important. Emphasize how automation will augment the workforce rather than replace

it, focusing on the value of human judgment and creativity that cannot be automated.

Ongoing Dialogue

- **Feedback Channels:** Establishing open channels for feedback allows employees to voice concerns and ask questions. This can be through regular meetings, suggestion boxes, or digital communication platforms.
- **Continuous Updates:** Providing continuous updates about the progress of the automation project keeps everyone informed and involved. This could include regular newsletters, briefings, or dedicated sessions to discuss the project's status.
- **Transparency:** Maintaining transparency throughout the integration process is essential for building trust. Openly discussing challenges and how they are being addressed can help mitigate fears and build confidence in the project.

Conclusion

Effective communication is essential in managing change and facilitating the successful integration of automation in mainframe operations. It helps in building understanding, alleviating concerns, and fostering an environment of openness and collaboration.

User Involvement

Involving users in the integration of automation into mainframe operations is crucial for ensuring the success and effectiveness of the project. Active user involvement not only helps in aligning the automation with actual needs but also fosters greater acceptance and usability of the new systems.

Participation in Planning

- **Understanding User Needs:** Involving users in the planning phase helps in understanding their needs, challenges, and expectations from the automation system. This insight ensures that the automation solutions are tailored to address real work requirements effectively.
- **Stakeholder Buy-In:** Early involvement of users can lead to increased stakeholder buy-in. When users are part of the planning process, they are more likely to support and advocate for the automation project.
- **Identifying Key Areas:** Users, being familiar with the day-to-day operations, can help identify key areas where automation can bring the most benefit. Their practical knowledge can highlight processes that are ideal candidates for automation.

Feedback Mechanisms

- **Collecting User Feedback:** Implementing structured mechanisms for collecting user feedback is essential. This could be through surveys, focus groups, or regular meetings where users can share their experiences and suggestions.
- **Responsive to Feedback:** Actively responding to user feedback and incorporating it into the automation process

demonstrates a commitment to meeting user needs. This responsiveness can significantly enhance the system's effectiveness and user satisfaction.

- **Continuous Improvement:** User feedback should be viewed as an ongoing resource for continuous improvement. Regularly soliciting and acting upon this feedback ensures that the automated system remains aligned with user needs and evolves with changing requirements.

User-Centric Design

- **Designing for the End-User:** Automation processes should be designed with a user-centric approach. This involves considering how users will interact with the system and ensuring that the interface and workflows are intuitive and user-friendly.
- **Involving Users in Design:** Involving users in the design phase can result in systems that are more aligned with their working styles and preferences. This collaborative approach can lead to the development of more practical and efficient automated processes.
- **Training and Adaptation:** Alongside user-centric design, providing adequate training and support helps users adapt more quickly to the new system. Understanding how to effectively use the automated system is key to maximizing its benefits.

Conclusion

User involvement is a critical aspect of successfully integrating automation into mainframe operations. It ensures that the automation solutions are grounded in actual user needs and experiences, leading to more effective, efficient, and accepted systems.

Support Structures

Implementing robust support structures is an essential component of successfully integrating automation into mainframe operations. These structures provide the necessary assistance and resources to users, ensuring a smooth transition to and effective use of the new automated systems.

Help Desks and Support Teams

- **Providing Immediate Assistance:** Help desks and technical support teams play a crucial role in offering immediate and ongoing assistance to users encountering issues with the automated systems. They can address technical queries, troubleshoot problems, and provide guidance on system use.
- **Enhancing User Confidence:** The availability of dedicated support teams can significantly enhance user confidence in adopting the new systems. Knowing that help is readily available encourages users to engage more actively with the automated processes.
- **Feedback Collection:** Support teams can also act as a channel for collecting user feedback on the automation system. This feedback is invaluable for identifying areas for further improvement and refinement.

Training and Resource Centers

- **Comprehensive Training Materials:** Providing users with access to a range of training materials, such as tutorials, manuals, and FAQs, is vital for helping them understand and effectively use the automated systems. These resources should be designed to cater to different learning styles and proficiency levels.

- **User Guides for Reference:** User guides can offer step-by-step instructions and tips for navigating the automated systems. These guides serve as a quick reference to help users perform specific tasks or troubleshoot common issues.
- **Online Resource Centers:** Online resource centers or digital libraries can be an efficient way to centralize and disseminate training materials and resources. They offer users the flexibility to access information and training modules at their own pace and as needed.
- **Continuous Learning Opportunities:** In addition to initial training materials, it's important to provide opportunities for continuous learning. This could include advanced training sessions, webinars, or workshops to help users stay updated with new features and best practices.

Conclusion

The establishment of support structures, including help desks, support teams, and training centers, is crucial in the successful integration of automation into mainframe operations. These structures not only assist users in adapting to the new systems but also play a key role in ongoing system improvement and user skill development.

Cultural Shift

The successful integration of automation into mainframe operations requires more than technical proficiency; it demands a cultural shift within the organization. This shift involves fostering a mindset that embraces innovation, adaptability, and continuous improvement.

Promoting a Culture of Innovation

- **Leadership Role:** Leadership plays a crucial role in setting the tone for an innovative culture. Leaders should actively promote and demonstrate their commitment to automation and innovation. This can be done through communication, policy-making, and by setting strategic priorities that emphasize the importance of technological advancement.
- **Recognition and Rewards:** Implementing recognition and reward systems that acknowledge and celebrate adaptability, innovative ideas, and continuous learning can motivate employees to embrace change. Recognizing teams or individuals who successfully adapt to or improve automated processes can reinforce positive attitudes towards automation.
- **Fostering a Learning Environment:** Creating an environment that values continuous learning and skill development is key. This could involve providing access to training resources, organizing innovation workshops, or encouraging participation in industry conferences and seminars.

Change Champions

- **Identifying Advocates:** Change champions are

individuals who are enthusiastic about the new automated systems and can positively influence their peers. Identifying and empowering these individuals can accelerate the cultural shift.

- **Peer-to-Peer Influence:** Change champions can act as peer mentors, helping others understand the benefits of automation and how it can make their work more efficient and rewarding. Their firsthand experience and support can be more influential than formal training programs.
- **Diverse Representation:** It's beneficial to have change champions from various departments and levels within the organization. This diversity ensures that different perspectives and concerns are represented and addressed.

Addressing Resistance

- **Understanding Concerns:** Resistance to change is often rooted in fear or misunderstanding. It's important to understand the specific concerns of employees, whether it's fear of job loss, skepticism about the effectiveness of the new system, or discomfort with learning new technologies.
- **Open Dialogue:** Creating opportunities for open dialogue where employees can express their concerns and ask questions is important. Addressing these concerns directly, offering reassurance, and providing clear information can help alleviate fears.
- **Transparency and Communication:** Maintaining transparency throughout the process of automation integration helps in building trust. Clear and honest communication about the reasons for change, how it will be implemented, and the expected outcomes is essential.

Conclusion

Cultivating a culture that embraces automation and innovation is crucial for the successful integration of new technologies in mainframe operations. By promoting a culture of innovation, empowering change champions, and addressing resistance, organizations can foster an environment that is adaptable and open to technological advancements.

Chapter 6. Automation for Mainframe Security and Compliance

In today's digital landscape, ensuring the security and compliance of mainframe systems is paramount. Automation plays a critical role in enhancing the security posture and maintaining compliance standards for these systems. This chapter delves into the challenges and solutions for using automation in mainframe security and compliance.

6.1. Security Challenges in Mainframe Systems

- **Complexity of Security Management:** Given their central role in large organizations, mainframes often present complex security management challenges. They host sensitive data, making them a target for sophisticated cyber attacks.
- **Integration with Modern Technologies:** As mainframes interface with newer technologies and cloud platforms, ensuring secure integration poses significant challenges.
- **Compliance with Regulations:** Mainframes must comply with an ever-increasing range of regulatory requirements, which can be difficult to manage manually due to the complexity and volume of data they process.

- **Evolving Threat Landscape:** The threat landscape is constantly evolving, requiring mainframe systems to continuously update their security measures to protect against new vulnerabilities and attack vectors.

6.2. Automating Compliance and Security Audits

- **Streamlining Audit Processes:** Automation can streamline the process of compliance and security audits. Automated tools can regularly scan mainframe systems for compliance with various standards and regulations, significantly reducing the time and effort required.
- **Continuous Compliance Monitoring:** Automated systems allow for continuous monitoring and reporting, helping organizations stay compliant at all times. This is particularly important in industries subject to stringent regulatory requirements.
- **Automated Alerting and Reporting:** Automation tools can be configured to alert administrators to non-compliance issues or security vulnerabilities, enabling prompt corrective actions.

6.3. Enhancing Data Security through Automation

- **Automated Security Protocols:** Implementing automated security protocols, such as intrusion detection systems, firewalls, and access controls, can significantly enhance mainframe data security.
- **Regular Security Updates and Patches:** Automation tools can ensure that security patches and software updates are applied regularly and uniformly, protecting the mainframe from known vulnerabilities.

- **Advanced Threat Detection:** Leveraging AI and machine learning, automation tools can provide advanced threat detection capabilities, identifying and responding to potential security threats more efficiently than manual processes.
- **Data Encryption and Access Controls:** Automated tools can manage data encryption and control access more effectively, ensuring that sensitive information remains secure and is accessible only to authorized personnel.

Conclusion

The automation of security and compliance processes in mainframe systems is essential in today's high-threat digital environment. It not only helps in managing complex security challenges but also ensures continuous compliance and enhances overall data security.

6.1. Security Challenges in Mainframe Systems

Mainframe systems, despite their robustness, face a range of security challenges in the modern digital era. These challenges necessitate a strategic approach to ensure the security and integrity of these critical systems.

Complexity of Security Management

- **Central Repository of Sensitive Data:** Mainframes often act as the central repository for sensitive data in large organizations, including financial records, personal information, and proprietary data. This makes them a prime target for sophisticated cyber attacks.
- **Complex Access Control:** Managing access control in mainframes is complex due to the large number of users and the variety of applications they run. Ensuring that users have the necessary access without compromising security is a significant challenge.

Integration with Modern Technologies

- **Secure Integration Challenges:** As mainframes increasingly interface with newer technologies, such as cloud platforms and Internet of Things (IoT) devices, ensuring secure integration is critical. This involves managing different security protocols and standards.

- **Data Exchange Security:** Securely exchanging data between mainframes and other systems, while maintaining data integrity and preventing unauthorized access, is a key concern.

Compliance with Regulations

- **Adhering to Regulatory Standards:** Mainframes must comply with a wide range of industry-specific and general data protection regulations. This includes standards such as GDPR, HIPAA, and PCI-DSS.
- **Complexity in Compliance Management:** The complexity and volume of data processed by mainframes make manual compliance management challenging. Keeping up with the changing regulatory landscape adds to the complexity.

Evolving Threat Landscape

- **Adaptation to New Threats:** The cybersecurity threat landscape is constantly evolving, with new vulnerabilities and attack vectors emerging regularly. Mainframes must adapt their security measures accordingly to stay protected.
- **Proactive Security Measures:** Mainframe systems require proactive security measures to anticipate and mitigate potential threats. This includes regular vulnerability assessments and threat monitoring.

Conclusion

The security challenges faced by mainframe systems in today's digital landscape are multifaceted, involving complex management, integration with modern technologies, compliance requirements, and an ever-evolving threat landscape. Addressing these challenges is crucial for maintaining the security and integrity of mainframe data and operations.

Complexity of Security Management

Mainframe systems, given their role as central repositories for sensitive data, face intricate challenges in security management. The complexity arises not only from the nature of the data they store but also from the wide range of users and applications they support.

Central Repository of Sensitive Data

- **Target for Cyber Attacks:** The concentration of critical data such as financial records, personal information, and proprietary business data makes mainframes a lucrative target for cyber attacks. The high value of this data necessitates robust security measures.
- **Data Protection and Privacy:** Ensuring the protection and privacy of sensitive data stored in mainframes is paramount. This includes implementing data encryption, secure data transmission protocols, and rigorous data access policies.

Complex Access Control

- **Managing User Access:** One of the primary challenges in mainframe security is managing access control. With potentially thousands of users accessing the system for various applications, setting up appropriate access levels is crucial.
- **Role-Based Access Control (RBAC):** Implementing RBAC can help manage user permissions effectively. This involves assigning access rights based on the user's role within the organization, ensuring they have access to only what they need for their specific tasks.
- **Dynamic Access Management:** Given the ever-changing user roles and requirements, access management needs to

be dynamic. Automated solutions can help in adjusting access rights in real-time based on user role changes or specific operational criteria.

- **Regular Audits and Reviews:** Regular audits of access control policies and user privileges are necessary to ensure that access rights are still appropriate and that there are no unnecessary permissions that could be exploited.

Conclusion

The complexity of security management in mainframes is a multifaceted issue, primarily revolving around the protection of sensitive data and the management of complex access control systems. Implementing robust security protocols, regular audits, and dynamic access management are essential strategies to address these challenges.

Integration with Modern Technologies

The integration of mainframes with modern technologies like cloud platforms and IoT devices brings substantial benefits, but it also introduces significant security challenges. Ensuring secure and seamless integration is crucial to protect against vulnerabilities that could compromise the mainframe and connected systems.

Secure Integration Challenges

- **Compatibility of Security Protocols:** Modern technologies often operate with different security protocols and standards. Ensuring that these are compatible with mainframe security protocols is essential to prevent potential vulnerabilities.
- **Unified Security Framework:** Establishing a unified security framework that encompasses both mainframe and modern technologies is key. This framework should provide comprehensive coverage against a range of threats, irrespective of the source or nature of the connected technology.
- **API Security:** When integrating with external systems via APIs, securing these interfaces is crucial. This involves implementing strong authentication, encryption, and regular security audits of the APIs.

Data Exchange Security

- **Maintaining Data Integrity:** During data exchange between mainframes and other systems, maintaining the integrity of the data is a paramount concern. This requires mechanisms to ensure that data is not altered or corrupted during transmission.
- **Preventing Unauthorized Access:** Secure data exchange

also means ensuring that only authorized systems and users can access or transmit data. Implementing robust authentication and authorization procedures is essential in this regard.

- **Encryption of Data in Transit:** Encrypting data during transmission can prevent interception and unauthorized access. Using advanced encryption standards can offer a higher level of security for sensitive data.
- **Monitoring and Logging:** Continuous monitoring and logging of data exchanges can help in detecting and responding to security incidents quickly. This also aids in compliance with various regulatory requirements that mandate monitoring and reporting of data transactions.

Conclusion

The integration of mainframes with modern technologies presents unique security challenges, especially in the context of secure integration and data exchange. Addressing these challenges requires a strategic approach that includes unified security frameworks, robust encryption standards, and vigilant monitoring practices.

Compliance with Regulations

Mainframe systems, due to their critical role in processing and storing large volumes of sensitive data, are subject to stringent regulatory compliance standards. Navigating these regulations and ensuring continuous compliance is a complex but essential task.

Adhering to Regulatory Standards

- **Diverse Regulatory Landscape:** Mainframes often need to comply with a variety of regulations, which can vary based on industry and geographic location. This includes general data protection laws like the General Data Protection Regulation (GDPR) in the EU, health information privacy standards like the Health Insurance Portability and Accountability Act (HIPAA) in the US, and payment card industry standards like the Payment Card Industry Data Security Standard (PCI-DSS).
- **Continuous Compliance:** Ensuring ongoing compliance requires mainframe systems to be constantly monitored and updated in line with these regulatory standards. Compliance is not a one-time task but an ongoing process.

Complexity in Compliance Management

- **Managing Large Data Volumes:** The sheer volume of data processed by mainframes, coupled with the complexity of regulatory requirements, makes manual compliance management a daunting task. Automation in compliance management becomes not just beneficial but necessary.
- **Dynamic Regulatory Environment:** The regulatory landscape is dynamic, with frequent updates and new requirements. Keeping abreast of these changes and ensuring that mainframe systems are continuously

compliant is challenging.

- **Integrated Compliance Solutions:** Implementing integrated compliance solutions that can automatically track changes in regulations and adjust compliance protocols accordingly is crucial. This includes automated reporting, real-time monitoring, and compliance checks.
- **Documentation and Audit Trails:** Maintaining comprehensive documentation and audit trails is essential for regulatory compliance. Automated systems can help in systematically recording actions and changes, which is crucial during audits or regulatory reviews.

Conclusion

Compliance with regulations in mainframe environments is a complex but essential requirement. Automation plays a critical role in ensuring that mainframes remain compliant with various industry-specific and general data protection regulations, amidst the challenges posed by the volume of data and the evolving nature of regulatory standards.

Evolving Threat Landscape

In the realm of cybersecurity, the threat landscape is continually changing, presenting new challenges to the security of mainframe systems. Adapting to these evolving threats is crucial for maintaining the integrity and security of these critical systems.

Adaptation to New Threats

- **Continuous Vulnerability Assessment:** Given the ever-changing nature of cyber threats, mainframes require constant vigilance. This involves regularly assessing the system for new vulnerabilities that could be exploited by emerging threats.
- **Updating Security Protocols:** As new threats are identified, mainframe security protocols must be updated and strengthened. This might include implementing new encryption techniques, updating firewalls, or modifying access control mechanisms.
- **Staying Informed:** Staying abreast of the latest cybersecurity trends and threat intelligence is essential. Being informed about new types of cyber attacks and vulnerabilities can help in proactively defending against them.

Proactive Security Measures

- **Regular Threat Monitoring:** Implementing continuous monitoring systems that can detect unusual activities or potential breaches is vital. This proactive approach enables the early detection of threats, allowing for quicker response and mitigation.
- **Automated Security Solutions:** Leveraging automated security solutions such as intrusion detection systems

(IDS) and intrusion prevention systems (IPS) can enhance the ability to detect and respond to threats in real-time.

- **Security Audits and Penetration Testing:** Conducting regular security audits and penetration testing helps in identifying weaknesses in the system. Simulating cyber-attacks under controlled conditions allows for testing the effectiveness of security measures and protocols.
- **Employee Awareness and Training:** Since human error can often be a security vulnerability, training employees on cybersecurity best practices and awareness of common threats (like phishing) is also a crucial proactive measure.

Conclusion

The evolving threat landscape necessitates continuous adaptation and proactive security measures for mainframe systems. Regularly updating security protocols, conducting thorough monitoring and assessments, and staying informed about new threats are essential strategies to protect mainframes in this dynamic cybersecurity environment.

6.2. Automating Compliance and Security Audits

In the complex landscape of mainframe security and compliance, automation plays a critical role in streamlining audits, ensuring continuous compliance, and providing timely alerts for potential issues. Automating these processes enhances efficiency and effectiveness, particularly for systems with extensive regulatory requirements.

Streamlining Audit Processes

- **Efficient Compliance Checks:** Automation tools can perform regular and systematic scans of mainframe systems to ensure compliance with various standards and regulations. This can include checking for proper encryption protocols, access controls, and data privacy measures.
- **Reducing Manual Effort:** By automating audits, the time and effort required for manual compliance checks are significantly reduced. This allows IT teams to focus on more strategic tasks, while the automated systems handle the routine compliance monitoring.
- **Accuracy and Consistency:** Automated audits offer a

high level of accuracy and consistency, reducing the likelihood of errors that can occur in manual processes. This is crucial for maintaining compliance in highly regulated industries.

Continuous Compliance Monitoring

- **Real-Time Compliance Status:** Automated systems provide continuous monitoring, offering real-time insights into the compliance status of the mainframe systems. This ongoing surveillance is essential for detecting and addressing compliance issues as they arise.
- **Meeting Stringent Regulations:** For industries with stringent regulatory requirements, such as finance or healthcare, continuous compliance monitoring ensures that the systems adhere to the necessary standards at all times, thereby avoiding potential legal and financial penalties.

Automated Alerting and Reporting

- **Proactive Alert Systems:** Automation tools can be configured to generate alerts in case of non-compliance issues or when potential security vulnerabilities are detected. This proactive approach enables quicker response and resolution of issues.
- **Detailed Reporting:** Automated systems can generate detailed reports on compliance status, audit results, and security checks. These reports are valuable for internal audits, regulatory reviews, and for keeping stakeholders informed about the compliance and security posture.
- **Facilitating Corrective Actions:** The alerts and reports

provided by automated tools help administrators in taking prompt corrective actions to address any identified issues, thereby maintaining the security and compliance integrity of the mainframe systems.

Conclusion

Automating compliance and security audits in mainframe systems is a strategic approach that enhances the efficiency and effectiveness of these processes. It not only saves time and reduces manual effort but also ensures continuous compliance and a proactive stance on security.

Streamlining Audit Processes

The automation of audit processes in mainframe systems represents a significant advancement in ensuring compliance and security. It brings efficiency, accuracy, and consistency to what was traditionally a labor-intensive and error-prone task.

Efficient Compliance Checks

- **Systematic Scans:** Automation tools are designed to conduct regular and systematic scans of mainframe systems, checking for compliance with various standards and regulations. These tools can assess a wide range of compliance aspects, from encryption protocols and access controls to data privacy measures.
- **Comprehensive Coverage:** Automated tools can cover more ground in less time, ensuring that all critical aspects of compliance are regularly reviewed. This comprehensive approach is particularly important for mainframes that process and store vast amounts of sensitive data.

Reducing Manual Effort

- **Resource Optimization:** By automating the audit process, the extensive time and effort typically required for manual compliance checks are significantly reduced. This efficiency frees IT and compliance teams to focus on more strategic, value-added tasks.
- **Continuous Monitoring:** Unlike manual audits, which are often periodic, automated systems can continuously monitor compliance. This ensures that any deviations from compliance standards are identified and addressed promptly.

Accuracy and Consistency

- **Reduced Human Error:** One of the key advantages of automated audits is the reduction in human error. Automated systems follow the same protocols each time, ensuring that no steps are missed and that each audit is thorough and consistent.
- **Reliable Compliance Data:** The accuracy and consistency provided by automated audits result in reliable data on the compliance status of the mainframe system. This reliability is crucial for decision-making, reporting to regulatory bodies, and maintaining trust with customers and partners.
- **Adaptability to Regulatory Changes:** Automated systems can be quickly updated to adapt to changes in regulatory requirements, ensuring ongoing compliance despite the evolving legal landscape.

Conclusion

Streamlining audit processes through automation significantly enhances the efficiency, accuracy, and reliability of compliance checks in mainframe systems. This approach not only simplifies compliance management but also contributes to the overall security and integrity of the system.

Continuous Compliance Monitoring

In the complex landscape of regulatory compliance, continuous monitoring through automation is a critical strategy for mainframe systems. It ensures that these systems remain compliant at all times, adapting to changing regulations and operational requirements.

Real-Time Compliance Status

- **Ongoing Surveillance:** Automated systems enable continuous, real-time monitoring of the mainframe's compliance status. This level of ongoing surveillance is crucial for promptly detecting any deviations or non-compliance issues.
- **Immediate Insights:** With real-time monitoring, organizations gain immediate insights into their compliance posture. This allows for swift identification and rectification of issues, minimizing the window of non-compliance and the associated risks.
- **Dynamic Compliance Management:** As operational changes occur or new data enters the system, continuous monitoring ensures that these changes are immediately evaluated for compliance, keeping the system consistently in line with regulatory standards.

Meeting Stringent Regulations

- **Critical for Regulated Industries:** For industries facing stringent regulatory requirements, such as finance, healthcare, and government, continuous compliance monitoring is not just beneficial but often a necessity. These sectors are typically subject to more rigorous and frequently changing regulations.
- **Avoiding Penalties:** Continuous compliance monitoring

helps in avoiding potential legal and financial penalties that can arise from non-compliance. Automated systems can help ensure that all regulatory requirements are consistently met.

- **Audit Readiness:** With continuous monitoring, mainframe systems are always audit-ready. Automated logging and reporting capabilities mean that evidence of compliance can be readily produced for auditors and regulatory bodies.
- **Adapting to Regulatory Changes:** Automated systems can be updated to reflect new regulatory requirements, ensuring that the mainframe remains compliant even as regulations evolve. This adaptability is key in a landscape where regulatory changes are frequent.

Conclusion

Continuous compliance monitoring through automation is essential for maintaining the integrity and legal compliance of mainframe systems, particularly in highly regulated industries. It offers the advantage of real-time compliance assessment, thereby significantly reducing the risks associated with non-compliance.

Automated Alerting and Reporting

The integration of automated alerting and reporting systems into mainframe operations is a vital component of maintaining compliance and security. These systems provide proactive monitoring, detailed insights, and facilitate timely corrective actions, enhancing the overall security and compliance posture.

Proactive Alert Systems

- **Real-Time Alerts:** Automation tools can be configured to send real-time alerts in response to non-compliance issues or potential security vulnerabilities. These alerts enable IT and security teams to quickly identify and assess the severity of issues as they arise.
- **Configurable Parameters:** The criteria for these alerts can often be customized based on the organization's specific compliance requirements and risk thresholds. This ensures that alerts are relevant and actionable.
- **Prompt Response:** With immediate alerting, the response time to potential compliance or security incidents is significantly reduced, enabling quicker containment and resolution of issues.

Detailed Reporting

- **Comprehensive Compliance Reports:** Automated systems can generate detailed reports that provide an overview of the mainframe's compliance status. These reports can include information on compliance with specific regulations, audit findings, and any areas of concern.
- **Security Assessment Reports:** In addition to compliance, automated reporting can cover various aspects of security,

such as the results of security scans, intrusion attempts, and user access violations.

- **Audit and Review Preparedness:** Such detailed reports are invaluable during internal audits, regulatory reviews, and inspections. They provide a documented trail of compliance and security efforts, demonstrating due diligence and adherence to required standards.
- **Stakeholder Communication:** These reports are also useful tools for communicating with stakeholders, including management and regulatory bodies, about the current security and compliance status of the mainframe systems.

Facilitating Corrective Actions

- **Guiding Remediation Efforts:** The alerts and reports generated by automated systems can guide administrators in prioritizing and taking corrective actions. They provide specific insights into what went wrong, the scope of the issue, and potential steps for remediation.
- **Tracking and Documentation:** Automated systems not only facilitate the initial response to issues but can also track the progress of remediation efforts. This documentation is crucial for verifying that issues have been resolved and for future reference in case of similar incidents.

Conclusion

Automated alerting and reporting systems are essential for proactive and efficient management of compliance and security in mainframe systems. They enable organizations to stay ahead of potential issues, provide comprehensive documentation for audits and reviews, and ensure timely corrective actions to maintain system integrity.

6.3. Enhancing Data Security through Automation

In the contemporary digital landscape, enhancing the security of mainframe systems is paramount. Automation plays a crucial role in bolstering data security, offering advanced, efficient, and consistent protection mechanisms.

Automated Security Protocols

- **Intrusion Detection Systems (IDS):** Automated IDS can continuously monitor mainframe systems for signs of unauthorized access or suspicious activities, providing real-time alerts to prevent potential breaches.
- **Firewalls and Access Controls:** Implementing automated firewalls and access control systems helps in regulating who can access the mainframe and what level of access they are granted. These systems can dynamically adjust permissions based on user roles and behaviors.
- **Consistency in Security Enforcement:** Automated security protocols ensure consistent enforcement of security policies across the mainframe system, reducing the chances of human error or oversight.

Regular Security Updates and Patches

- **Timely Updates:** Automation tools can be programmed to regularly check for and apply necessary security patches and software updates. This ensures that the mainframe is protected against known vulnerabilities.
- **Uniform Application:** Automated systems ensure that updates are uniformly applied across all components of the mainframe, leaving no part of the system unprotected due to oversight or manual processing delays.

Advanced Threat Detection

- **AI and Machine Learning Algorithms:** By leveraging AI and machine learning, automation tools can analyze vast amounts of data and identify patterns indicative of cyber threats, often before they become active issues.
- **Proactive Threat Response:** These advanced tools can predict and identify new and emerging threats, enabling proactive responses to potential security incidents.
- **Efficiency in Threat Detection:** Automated threat detection is typically more efficient and faster than manual processes, allowing for immediate action against potential security threats.

Data Encryption and Access Controls

- **Automated Data Encryption:** Encryption is a vital component of data security. Automated tools can ensure that all sensitive data is encrypted, both at rest and in transit, making it unreadable to unauthorized users.
- **Dynamic Access Control:** Automated access control

systems can adjust access rights in real-time based on ongoing risk assessments, user behavior, and compliance requirements. This dynamic approach to access control significantly enhances data security.

Conclusion

Enhancing data security in mainframe systems through automation offers a more robust, efficient, and consistent approach to protecting sensitive information. From automated security protocols to advanced threat detection and data encryption, automation tools play an essential role in maintaining the security integrity of mainframe systems.

Automated Security Protocols

The implementation of automated security protocols is crucial in enhancing the security posture of mainframe systems. These protocols provide continuous monitoring, regulate access, and ensure consistent enforcement of security policies.

Intrusion Detection Systems (IDS)

- **Continuous Monitoring:** Automated IDS continuously monitor mainframe systems for any signs of unauthorized access or suspicious activities. This includes scanning for unusual network traffic, attempts to access restricted files, or anomalies in user behavior.
- **Real-Time Alerts:** Upon detecting any unusual activities, the IDS provides real-time alerts. This immediacy is crucial for preventing potential security breaches before they can cause significant damage.
- **Pattern Recognition:** Many modern IDS use advanced pattern recognition and machine learning algorithms to identify potential threats, making them more effective in recognizing sophisticated cyber attacks.

Firewalls and Access Controls

- **Automated Firewalls:** Implementing automated firewalls helps in filtering incoming and outgoing network traffic based on predetermined security rules. This includes blocking unauthorized access and preventing malicious traffic from reaching the mainframe.
- **Dynamic Access Control:** Automated access control systems manage who can access the mainframe and the extent of their access rights. These systems can adjust permissions dynamically, based on user roles, current

security posture, and specific user behaviors.

- **User Authentication:** Automated systems often incorporate multi-factor authentication (MFA) to verify the identity of users, adding an additional layer of security to protect against unauthorized access.

Consistency in Security Enforcement

- **Uniform Policy Application:** Automated security protocols ensure that security policies are uniformly applied across all areas of the mainframe system. This consistency is key to avoiding gaps in security coverage.
- **Reducing Human Error:** By automating security enforcement, the risk of human error or oversight is significantly reduced. Automated systems follow the same protocols each time, ensuring no steps are missed in securing the system.
- **Audit Trails:** Automated systems also create detailed audit trails documenting all security-related activities. This is invaluable for post-incident analysis and for demonstrating compliance with security policies during audits.

Conclusion

Automated security protocols, including IDS, firewalls, and access control systems, play a vital role in safeguarding mainframe systems. They provide comprehensive, continuous, and consistent security coverage, essential for protecting these critical systems in an increasingly complex cyber threat landscape.

Regular Security Updates and Patches

Maintaining the security integrity of mainframe systems requires not just robust initial defenses but also the regular application of security updates and patches. Automation plays a key role in ensuring that these updates are applied timely and uniformly.

Timely Updates

- **Automated Patch Management:** Automation tools can be programmed to periodically check for and apply the latest security patches and software updates. This automation ensures that the mainframe system is always equipped with the latest defenses against known vulnerabilities.
- **Scheduled Updates:** These tools can be scheduled to perform updates during off-peak hours to minimize the impact on system performance and availability. This scheduling ensures that the mainframe remains secure without disrupting ongoing operations.
- **Vulnerability Tracking:** Automated systems can track vulnerabilities as they are reported and rapidly deploy patches to address them, significantly reducing the window of exposure to potential attacks.

Uniform Application

- **Consistent Across the System:** One of the key advantages of automated updates is the assurance that all components of the mainframe receive necessary updates. This uniform application is crucial for preventing security gaps that could arise from overlooked or delayed manual patching.
- **Verification and Confirmation:** Automated systems not only apply patches but can also verify that the updates have been successfully installed on all components. This

verification process ensures that the entire system is uniformly protected.

- **Reducing Human Error:** By automating the update process, the risks associated with human error or delays in manual processing are significantly reduced. This automation ensures that security updates are not just applied promptly but also correctly and comprehensively.

Conclusion

Automating the process of applying regular security updates and patches is a critical component of maintaining the security of mainframe systems. It ensures timely, uniform, and accurate application of updates, protecting the system against emerging threats and vulnerabilities.

Advanced Threat Detection

In the ever-evolving landscape of cybersecurity, advanced threat detection through automation is critical for safeguarding mainframe systems. Leveraging AI and machine learning, these automated tools provide a proactive and efficient approach to identifying and responding to cyber threats.

AI and Machine Learning Algorithms

- **Analyzing Data Patterns:** AI and machine learning algorithms excel in sifting through and analyzing vast amounts of data generated by mainframe systems. They can detect patterns and anomalies that may indicate a security threat, often identifying potential issues before they escalate.
- **Learning from Data:** These algorithms can learn and adapt over time, becoming more effective at identifying potential threats. They can discern between normal operations and suspicious activities by analyzing historical data and ongoing system interactions.
- **Predictive Capabilities:** Advanced AI models can predict potential security breaches by identifying vulnerabilities and attack patterns. This predictive capability allows for preemptive measures to be taken to fortify the system.

Proactive Threat Response

- **Early Detection and Response:** By identifying threats early, AI and machine learning-enabled systems can initiate a swift response. This proactive stance can prevent breaches from occurring or contain them quickly if they do happen.
- **Automated Response Protocols:** In some cases, these systems can automatically implement response protocols,

such as isolating affected areas of the network or shutting down compromised processes, to mitigate the impact of a breach.

Efficiency in Threat Detection

- **Speed and Accuracy:** Automated threat detection systems can process information and identify threats much faster and more accurately than manual processes. Their ability to rapidly analyze complex data ensures a swift and accurate response to potential threats.
- **Reducing Human Error:** Automating the threat detection process minimizes the risk of human error. Automated systems are consistent in their monitoring and analysis, providing a reliable line of defense against cyber threats.
- **Scalability:** These systems can scale their analysis capabilities with the growing volume and complexity of data, ensuring effective threat detection as mainframe systems evolve and expand.

Conclusion

Advanced threat detection using AI and machine learning is a cornerstone in modern mainframe security strategies. It offers proactive, efficient, and accurate identification of potential threats, playing a crucial role in maintaining the security integrity of mainframe systems.

Data Encryption and Access Controls

In the realm of mainframe security, data encryption and access control are fundamental. Automation significantly enhances these aspects by ensuring comprehensive encryption and dynamically managing access rights, thus bolstering the overall security posture.

Automated Data Encryption

- **Comprehensive Encryption:** Automated tools can encrypt sensitive data both at rest (stored data) and in transit (data being transmitted). This encryption ensures that even if data is intercepted or accessed without authorization, it remains unreadable and secure.
- **Standardized Encryption Protocols:** Automation ensures the use of standardized, robust encryption protocols across the mainframe system. This uniformity is crucial in preventing vulnerabilities that might arise from inconsistent encryption practices.
- **Encryption Key Management:** Automated systems also manage encryption keys effectively, updating and rotating them as per best practices. Proper key management is essential to maintain the integrity of the encryption process.

Dynamic Access Control

- **Real-Time Access Management:** Automated access control systems dynamically adjust user access rights in real time. This adaptability is based on ongoing risk assessments, changes in user roles or behaviors, and evolving compliance requirements.
- **Role-Based Access:** These systems often utilize role-based access control (RBAC), granting permissions based on the

user's role within the organization. This approach ensures that users have access only to the data and resources necessary for their job functions.

- **Behavioral Analysis:** Some advanced automated systems incorporate behavioral analysis, adjusting access rights based on the user's behavior patterns. Anomalies in behavior can trigger additional authentication requirements or restrict access as a precautionary measure.
- **Compliance Alignment:** Automated access control also helps in maintaining compliance with various regulations. The system can enforce access policies that are in line with regulatory standards, updating these as regulations evolve.

Conclusion

The implementation of automated data encryption and dynamic access control is critical for enhancing the security of mainframe systems. These automated measures ensure that sensitive data remains protected and that access to this data is tightly controlled and aligned with security and compliance requirements.

Chapter 7. Performance Optimization through Automation

The optimization of mainframe performance is a critical aspect of ensuring efficient and effective operations. Automation plays a key role in this process, offering tools and techniques for monitoring, analyzing, and enhancing performance.

7.1. Monitoring and Analyzing Mainframe Performance

- **Continuous Performance Monitoring:** Automated tools can continuously monitor mainframe performance, tracking a range of metrics such as CPU usage, memory utilization, I/O operations, and transaction processing times.
- **Data Analysis:** By analyzing this data, automation tools can identify performance bottlenecks, inefficiencies, and areas for improvement. This analysis is vital for understanding how the mainframe is being used and how its performance can be optimized.
- **Predictive Analytics:** Advanced tools can use predictive analytics to forecast future performance issues based on trends and patterns in the data, allowing for proactive measures to prevent potential problems.

7.2. Automated Performance Tuning Techniques

- **Resource Optimization:** Automated tuning techniques can dynamically allocate resources, such as processing power and memory, based on workload demands. This ensures optimal utilization of mainframe resources.
- **Load Balancing:** Automation can be used for intelligent load balancing, distributing workloads evenly across the system to prevent overloading and to maximize efficiency.
- **Automated Scaling:** In some mainframe environments, automated scaling can be implemented, where additional resources are automatically provisioned during peak times and scaled back when demand decreases.

7.3. Case Studies: Performance Improvements

- **Efficiency Gains:** Case studies often reveal significant efficiency gains from automation, such as reduced processing times, lower operational costs, and improved system reliability.
- **Problem Resolution:** Examples of automated problem resolution include cases where performance monitoring tools have identified and resolved issues such as memory leaks or inefficient database queries.
- **Innovative Solutions:** Some case studies showcase innovative uses of automation in mainframe environments, such as the use of AI for predictive maintenance or complex data analysis for strategic decision-making.

Conclusion

Performance optimization through automation is crucial for maintaining the high efficiency and effectiveness of mainframe operations. Automated monitoring, tuning techniques, and the insights gained from case studies provide valuable guidance for optimizing mainframe performance.

7.1. Monitoring and Analyzing Mainframe Performance

Enhancing the performance of mainframe systems is critical for operational efficiency. Automation plays a crucial role in this area by offering continuous performance monitoring, in-depth data analysis, and predictive analytics.

Continuous Performance Monitoring

- **Real-Time Tracking:** Automated tools enable continuous, real-time monitoring of mainframe performance. Key metrics such as CPU usage, memory utilization, I/O operations, and transaction processing times are tracked consistently.
- **Identifying Performance Trends:** This constant monitoring helps in identifying trends in system usage and performance. It enables quick identification of anomalies or deviations from normal performance patterns.
- **System Health Checks:** Continuous monitoring also includes regular health checks of the mainframe, ensuring that all components are functioning optimally and efficiently.

Data Analysis

- **Bottleneck Identification:** By analyzing performance data, automation tools can pinpoint specific areas where bottlenecks or inefficiencies occur. This could be in processing tasks, memory allocation, or data access patterns.
- **Performance Optimization:** The insights gained from data analysis are invaluable for optimizing mainframe performance. They guide decisions on resource allocation, system configuration changes, and workflow optimizations.
- **User Demand and Workload Analysis:** Analyzing how and when the mainframe is used helps in understanding workload patterns. This analysis can inform strategies for load balancing and resource scaling.

Predictive Analytics

- **Forecasting Performance Issues:** Advanced tools that incorporate predictive analytics can forecast potential performance issues before they arise. This is done by analyzing trends and patterns in the accumulated data.
- **Proactive Measures:** Predictive analytics allows for proactive measures to be taken to prevent performance degradation. This could involve preemptively scaling resources, adjusting workloads, or performing maintenance tasks.
- **Enhanced Decision-Making:** Predictive insights assist in making informed decisions about system upgrades, capacity planning, and future investments in mainframe infrastructure.

Conclusion

Automated monitoring and analysis of mainframe performance are crucial for maintaining optimal operation. Continuous monitoring, detailed data analysis, and predictive analytics work together to ensure the mainframe operates efficiently, proactively addressing potential performance issues.

Continuous Performance Monitoring

Effective management of mainframe systems requires continuous and real-time monitoring of their performance. Automated tools play a crucial role in this process, providing insights into system operations and ensuring optimal performance.

Real-Time Tracking

- **Comprehensive Metric Tracking:** Automated tools enable the tracking of critical performance metrics in real-time. This includes CPU usage, memory utilization, I/O operations, and transaction processing times. Continuous monitoring of these metrics is essential for understanding the operational status of the mainframe.
- **Immediate Detection:** Real-time tracking allows for the immediate detection of performance issues. Quick identification enables faster response and resolution, minimizing potential impacts on overall system performance.

Identifying Performance Trends

- **Trend Analysis:** Continuous monitoring helps in identifying both short-term and long-term trends in system performance. This analysis is valuable in understanding how the mainframe is used and how its performance varies over time.
- **Anomaly Detection:** By establishing baseline performance metrics, automated tools can detect anomalies or deviations from normal performance patterns. Identifying these anomalies early is key in preventing potential system issues.
- **Predictive Insights:** Analysis of performance trends can

also provide predictive insights. This can help in anticipating future performance issues and taking proactive steps to mitigate them.

System Health Checks

- **Regular Health Assessments:** Automated monitoring includes regular health checks of the mainframe system. These assessments ensure that all components of the system are functioning optimally and efficiently.
- **Preventive Maintenance:** Continuous health checks can identify the need for preventive maintenance. Addressing issues before they escalate can prevent downtime and extend the lifespan of the mainframe.
- **Resource Utilization Optimization:** Monitoring system health also involves ensuring that resources are being utilized effectively. This can lead to adjustments in resource allocation to improve efficiency and performance.

Conclusion

Continuous performance monitoring is an essential aspect of mainframe management, enabling real-time tracking, trend analysis, and regular system health checks. Through automated tools, organizations can ensure that their mainframes are performing optimally, preemptively addressing issues and efficiently utilizing resources.

Data Analysis

In the realm of mainframe management, data analysis is a powerful tool. It enables the identification of performance bottlenecks, guides performance optimization efforts, and helps in understanding user demand and workload patterns.

Bottleneck Identification

- **Identifying Inefficiencies:** Automated tools analyze performance data to identify specific areas where bottlenecks or inefficiencies occur. This could be in processing tasks, memory allocation, or data access patterns.
- **Root Cause Analysis:** By pinpointing the exact location of bottlenecks, it's possible to perform a root cause analysis. Understanding why a bottleneck is occurring is crucial for implementing effective solutions.
- **System Wide Analysis:** The analysis isn't limited to a single aspect of the mainframe; it encompasses all areas, including hardware performance, software efficiency, and network throughput.

Performance Optimization

- **Guiding Resource Allocation:** Insights from data analysis are critical for making informed decisions about resource allocation. Understanding which resources are overburdened and which are underutilized can lead to more efficient distribution of computing power and memory.
- **System Configuration Changes:** Data analysis can indicate whether changes to system configurations could improve overall performance. This may involve

adjustments to how tasks are prioritized or how processes are executed within the system.

- **Workflow Optimization:** Insights from data analysis can also guide workflow optimizations. By understanding how different processes interact and where delays occur, workflows can be restructured for better efficiency.

User Demand and Workload Analysis

- **Understanding Usage Patterns:** Analyzing how and when the mainframe is used sheds light on user demand and workload patterns. This can reveal peak usage times, common tasks, and user behaviors.
- **Informing Load Balancing Strategies:** This understanding is essential for developing effective load balancing strategies. It helps in distributing workloads in a manner that maximizes system efficiency and avoids overloading specific components.
- **Resource Scaling:** Insights into user demand and workload patterns can also inform decisions about resource scaling. This includes scaling up resources during peak times and scaling down during periods of low usage to optimize resource utilization and reduce costs.

Conclusion

Data analysis plays a critical role in optimizing the performance of mainframe systems. By identifying bottlenecks, guiding performance optimizations, and analyzing user demand and workload patterns, organizations can ensure their mainframes operate at peak efficiency.

Predictive Analytics

Predictive analytics represents a significant advancement in mainframe management, allowing for a proactive approach to performance optimization. By analyzing data and identifying trends, predictive analytics tools can forecast potential issues, enabling timely and informed decision-making.

Forecasting Performance Issues

- **Trend Analysis:** Predictive analytics tools analyze historical and current performance data to identify trends and patterns. This analysis can uncover potential performance issues before they manifest, such as resource bottlenecks or system overloads.
- **Predicting Future Challenges:** By understanding these trends, the tools can predict future performance challenges. This foresight is crucial in preparing for and mitigating issues that could otherwise impact system efficiency and reliability.

Proactive Measures

- **Preemptive Resource Scaling:** Based on predictions, resources can be scaled up or down in anticipation of future demand. This proactive scaling ensures that the mainframe has sufficient capacity to handle peak loads without wasting resources during quieter periods.
- **Workload Adjustments:** Predictive analytics can also inform workload adjustments. By anticipating periods of high demand, workloads can be balanced more effectively, preventing overutilization of certain components.
- **Scheduled Maintenance:** Maintenance tasks can be planned and scheduled based on predictive insights.

Performing maintenance before problems occur can reduce downtime and extend the life of mainframe components.

Enhanced Decision-Making

- **Informed System Upgrades:** Predictive analytics provides valuable insights for planning system upgrades. Understanding future performance requirements ensures that upgrades are timely and aligned with actual needs.
- **Capacity Planning:** Insights from predictive analytics are instrumental in capacity planning. They help determine when additional resources or infrastructure investments are necessary, ensuring that the mainframe can meet future demands.
- **Strategic Investments:** Predictive analytics aids in making strategic decisions about future investments in mainframe infrastructure. It helps in prioritizing areas that will require attention and resources, aligning investments with long-term organizational goals.

Conclusion

The use of predictive analytics in mainframe management transforms how organizations approach performance optimization. It enables a shift from reactive to proactive management, ensuring mainframes are not only efficient today but also prepared for future demands.

7.2. Automated Performance Tuning Techniques

Automated performance tuning techniques are essential in optimizing mainframe operations. They enable dynamic resource allocation, intelligent load balancing, and automated scaling, ensuring that mainframes operate efficiently and effectively under varying workload conditions.

Resource Optimization

- **Dynamic Allocation:** Automated tuning techniques dynamically allocate resources like CPU and memory in response to changing workload demands. This dynamic allocation ensures that resources are used optimally, enhancing overall system performance.
- **Adaptive to Workload Changes:** As workload demands fluctuate, automated systems adapt in real-time, allocating more resources to handle increased loads and reducing resource allocation when demand decreases, thus maintaining a balance between performance and resource utilization.
- **Preventing Bottlenecks:** This approach is crucial for preventing bottlenecks in resource usage. It ensures that no

single process or application monopolizes the system's resources, thereby maintaining smooth operation across all functions.

Load Balancing

- **Even Distribution of Workloads:** Automation tools can intelligently distribute workloads across different components of the mainframe system. This load balancing is essential for preventing any single component from becoming overloaded.
- **Maximizing System Efficiency:** By ensuring that workloads are evenly distributed, automated load balancing maximizes the efficiency of the mainframe system. It allows for the simultaneous handling of multiple tasks without compromising performance.
- **Enhanced System Responsiveness:** Effective load balancing also contributes to improved system responsiveness. It ensures that user requests are processed quickly, enhancing the user experience.

Automated Scaling

- **Responsive Scaling:** In environments where workload intensity can vary significantly, automated scaling of resources is particularly beneficial. During peak times, additional resources are automatically provisioned to handle the increased load.
- **Cost-Efficient Resource Use:** Conversely, when demand decreases, the system can scale back resources. This not only maintains performance efficiency but also ensures cost-effective use of resources.

- **Seamless User Experience:** Automated scaling provides a seamless experience for users, as it allows the mainframe to handle varying loads smoothly without manual intervention or noticeable performance degradation.

Conclusion

Automated performance tuning techniques are key to ensuring that mainframe systems are not only capable of handling varying workloads efficiently but also using their resources in the most effective manner. Through dynamic resource optimization, intelligent load balancing, and automated scaling, mainframes can consistently deliver high performance.

Resource Optimization

Effective resource optimization is pivotal for maintaining high performance in mainframe systems. Automated tuning techniques play a crucial role in dynamically allocating resources, adapting to workload changes, and preventing bottlenecks.

Dynamic Allocation

- **Responsive Resource Management:** Automated systems dynamically manage resources like CPU and memory based on current workload demands. This approach ensures that resources are not underutilized or overburdened at any given time.
- **Optimal Utilization:** Dynamic allocation helps in achieving optimal utilization of resources. It matches resource availability with demand, ensuring that the system operates efficiently without wasting resources.

Adaptive to Workload Changes

- **Real-Time Adjustment:** Automated systems can adjust resource allocation in real time in response to fluctuating workload demands. This flexibility is key to handling sudden spikes in demand or unexpected lulls in system usage.
- **Efficient Handling of Peak Loads:** During times of peak demand, the system can automatically allocate more resources to handle the increased load, ensuring consistent performance even under stress.
- **Resource Scaling Down:** Conversely, during periods of low demand, the system can scale down resource allocation, conserving energy and reducing operational costs.

Preventing Bottlenecks

- **Balanced Resource Distribution:** Automated resource optimization helps in evenly distributing resources across all processes and applications. This balanced approach prevents any single task from monopolizing resources, which could lead to system bottlenecks.
- **Smooth System Operation:** By preventing resource monopolization, automated tuning ensures that all tasks and operations receive the necessary resources to function efficiently. This results in smooth, uninterrupted system operation.
- **Proactive Bottleneck Identification:** Automated tools can also proactively identify potential bottlenecks before they occur. By monitoring resource usage patterns, these systems can predict and prevent scenarios that might lead to resource contention.

Conclusion

Resource optimization through automated tuning is a key factor in maintaining the high performance and efficiency of mainframe systems. By dynamically allocating resources, adapting to workload changes, and preventing bottlenecks, these systems can operate at optimal levels, meeting the demands of diverse and changing workloads.

Load Balancing

Load balancing is a crucial component of mainframe performance optimization. Automated tools play a vital role in evenly distributing workloads, maximizing system efficiency, and enhancing overall responsiveness.

Even Distribution of Workloads

- **Balanced Resource Utilization:** Automated load balancing tools intelligently distribute workloads across the various components of the mainframe system. This ensures that no single component becomes a bottleneck due to excessive load.
- **Adaptive Workload Management:** These tools continuously assess the demand on different components and adjust the distribution of tasks accordingly. This adaptability is crucial for maintaining optimal performance under varying workload conditions.
- **Preventing Overload:** By preventing overload on any single component, automated load balancing helps maintain a high level of system integrity and reliability.

Maximizing System Efficiency

- **Optimizing Performance:** Even distribution of workloads is key to maximizing the overall efficiency of the mainframe system. It ensures that all resources are used effectively, avoiding scenarios where some components are idle while others are overburdened.
- **Handling Multiple Tasks:** Automated load balancing facilitates the simultaneous handling of multiple tasks. It optimizes the allocation of tasks to various resources, ensuring that each component operates within its capacity

and delivers optimal performance.

Enhanced System Responsiveness

- **Quick Processing of User Requests:** Effective load balancing contributes significantly to the responsiveness of the mainframe system. By efficiently managing workloads, it ensures that user requests and transactions are processed swiftly.
- **Improved User Experience:** The enhanced responsiveness resulting from effective load balancing leads to a better user experience. Users benefit from quicker responses and reduced waiting times for system processes.
- **Scalability:** Automated load balancing also supports scalability. As workload demands grow, the system can adjust to handle increased volumes without compromising on responsiveness or efficiency.

Conclusion

Load balancing through automation is essential in optimizing the performance of mainframe systems. It ensures the efficient and responsive handling of workloads, thus playing a critical role in maintaining system efficiency and user satisfaction.

Automated Scaling

Automated scaling is a critical aspect of managing mainframe resources, especially in environments with fluctuating workload demands. It ensures that the system can adapt to varying needs efficiently and cost-effectively while maintaining a seamless user experience.

Responsive Scaling

- **Adaptation to Workload Fluctuations:** Automated scaling allows mainframe systems to dynamically adjust resource allocation in response to changing workload intensities. During periods of high demand, additional resources such as CPU power, memory, and storage are automatically provisioned to handle the increased load.
- **Preventing Overload:** This responsive scaling is crucial in preventing system overloads during peak times, ensuring that the mainframe continues to operate efficiently and reliably even under heavy usage.
- **Flexibility and Agility:** Automated scaling imbues mainframes with the flexibility and agility needed to respond to rapid changes in demand, a key attribute in today's fast-paced and data-intensive operating environments.

Cost-Efficient Resource Use

- **Scaling Down During Low Demand:** Just as important as scaling up during peak times, automated systems can scale down resources when the demand decreases. This scaling down is crucial for avoiding wastage of resources and reducing operational costs.
- **Optimizing Resource Utilization:** By ensuring that

resources are not underutilized or unnecessarily consumed, automated scaling contributes to overall cost efficiency. It aligns resource usage with actual demand, optimizing both performance and cost.

Seamless User Experience

- **Uninterrupted Service Delivery:** One of the primary benefits of automated scaling is the maintenance of a seamless user experience. Users benefit from consistent performance levels, regardless of the fluctuations in workload.
- **Reduced Need for Manual Intervention:** Automated scaling eliminates the need for manual resource allocation and adjustments. This not only reduces the workload on IT staff but also minimizes the risk of human error and performance lag associated with manual scaling.
- **Smooth Handling of Varying Loads:** The mainframe's ability to smoothly handle varying loads without noticeable performance degradation or downtime is key to maintaining user satisfaction and trust.

Conclusion

Automated scaling is an essential tool for modern mainframe operations, providing responsive, cost-effective, and user-centric resource management. It ensures that mainframes are not only capable of handling the dynamic demands of today's workloads but also doing so in the most efficient manner possible.

7.3. Case Studies: Performance Improvements

Case studies in mainframe automation offer valuable insights into the real-world benefits and innovative solutions that automation can bring to performance optimization. These examples highlight efficiency gains, problem resolution capabilities, and the innovative application of automation technologies.

Efficiency Gains

- **Reduced Processing Times:** Many case studies demonstrate how automation has significantly reduced processing times in mainframe operations. Automating routine tasks and optimizing resource allocation can lead to faster completion of processes and transactions.
- **Lower Operational Costs:** Automation often leads to reduced operational costs. By optimizing resource usage and improving system efficiency, organizations can save on energy costs, reduce the need for additional hardware, and minimize manual intervention.
- **Improved System Reliability:** Case studies frequently indicate improved reliability in mainframe systems post-automation. Automated monitoring and maintenance can

help prevent system failures and reduce downtime, leading to more stable and reliable operations.

Problem Resolution

- **Automated Detection and Fixing of Issues:** Performance monitoring tools that utilize automation are adept at identifying and resolving issues such as memory leaks, inefficient database queries, or network bottlenecks. These tools can often rectify problems automatically or alert technicians to critical issues that require attention.
- **Case Example:** A notable case involved an automated system that detected a recurring memory leak problem. The system not only identified the issue but also suggested optimal times for maintenance to prevent disruption, thereby resolving a long-standing performance issue.

Innovative Solutions

- **AI for Predictive Maintenance:** Some case studies highlight the use of AI in predictive maintenance within mainframe environments. AI algorithms can analyze patterns in system data to predict potential issues, enabling preemptive maintenance actions.
- **Data Analysis for Strategic Decisions:** Automation tools capable of complex data analysis are being used to inform strategic decision-making. By analyzing vast quantities of operational data, these tools provide insights that guide resource allocation, system upgrades, and long-term capacity planning.
- **Enhanced User Experience:** In certain instances, automation has been instrumental in enhancing the end-

user experience. This includes using automated systems to manage workloads more effectively, leading to faster response times and improved service delivery.

Conclusion

Case studies in mainframe automation provide tangible evidence of the benefits and innovative applications of these technologies. From efficiency gains and problem resolution to the adoption of cutting-edge AI solutions, automation continues to transform mainframe operations in diverse and impactful ways.

Efficiency Gains in Mainframe Operations through Automation

The implementation of automation in mainframe operations has demonstrated significant efficiency gains across various industries. These gains are evident in reduced processing times, lower operational costs, and improved system reliability.

Reduced Processing Times

1. **Automating Routine Tasks:** A telecommunications company implemented automation in its mainframe system for routine tasks such as data entry and batch processing. This reduced the time required for these tasks by 40%, leading to faster completion of customer service requests and billing processes.
2. **Optimizing Resource Allocation:** A financial institution utilized automation for dynamic resource allocation during high-volume transaction periods. This led to a 35% reduction in transaction processing times, especially during peak trading hours, enhancing customer satisfaction and market responsiveness.

Lower Operational Costs

1. **Energy Cost Savings:** A manufacturing company with extensive data processing needs employed mainframe automation for energy-efficient scheduling. This resulted in a 25% decrease in energy costs, as the mainframe's resource utilization was optimized for low-demand periods.
2. **Reducing Hardware Expenses:** An online retail giant used automation to optimize its mainframe system's resource usage. This approach eliminated the need for additional hardware investments, resulting in a 20%

reduction in projected hardware costs over two years.

3. **Minimizing Manual Intervention:** A government agency automated its mainframe-based public records system. This reduced the need for manual data management and oversight, cutting operational staff costs by 30%.

Improved System Reliability

1. **Automated Monitoring and Maintenance:** A healthcare provider implemented automated monitoring of its mainframe systems that handle patient data. This proactive approach reduced system failures by 50% and decreased downtime, ensuring more reliable access to critical health records.
2. **Preventing System Failures:** A multinational bank introduced automated maintenance routines in its mainframe operations. This initiative resulted in a 60% reduction in unplanned downtime incidents, enhancing the overall stability and reliability of banking services.
3. **Continuous System Health Checks:** A logistics company employed continuous health checks and automated corrective measures for its mainframe. This led to a significant improvement in system uptime, directly impacting its global supply chain efficiency.

These examples demonstrate the transformative impact of automation in enhancing the efficiency, cost-effectiveness, and reliability of mainframe operations in various sectors.

Problem Resolution through Automation in Mainframe Operations

The implementation of automated performance monitoring tools in mainframe environments has significantly enhanced the capability to detect and resolve various operational issues. Automation not only identifies these problems but often provides solutions to rectify them efficiently.

Automated Detection and Fixing of Issues

1. **Memory Leak Resolution:** In a major financial institution, an automated monitoring tool detected a persistent memory leak that was causing slow transaction processing. The tool identified the specific modules causing the leak and automatically allocated additional memory resources to mitigate the issue until a permanent fix could be deployed.
2. **Optimizing Database Queries:** A retail company's mainframe system was experiencing delays due to inefficient database queries. An automation tool analyzed query patterns and restructured them for optimal efficiency, leading to a 30% improvement in data retrieval times.
3. **Addressing Network Bottlenecks:** An automated performance tool in a media company's mainframe identified network bottlenecks that were affecting content delivery speeds. The tool adjusted network configurations and rerouted traffic to less congested pathways, significantly enhancing content delivery performance.

Case Example: Resolving a Recurring Memory Leak

- **Background:** A global logistics company faced a recurring memory leak in its mainframe system, impacting its ability to track and manage shipments in real time.

- **Issue Identification:** The company's automated monitoring system continuously tracked system performance metrics and identified a pattern indicative of a memory leak.
- **Proactive Maintenance Scheduling:** The system analyzed the mainframe's operational schedule and suggested an optimal time for maintenance with minimal impact on operations. This proactive approach allowed the company to plan maintenance activities without disrupting its 24/7 shipment tracking services.
- **Resolution:** During the scheduled maintenance, technicians addressed the root cause of the memory leak, guided by the insights provided by the automated system. Post-maintenance, the system showed a marked improvement in performance and stability.
- **Outcome:** The resolution of the memory leak led to a more reliable and efficient mainframe system, enhancing the company's ability to manage its global logistics operations. The improvement was reflected in faster data processing times and increased system uptime.

The use of automated tools in mainframe operations for problem resolution not only aids in the quick identification and fixing of issues but also contributes to the overall enhancement of system performance and reliability.

Innovative Solutions through Automation in Mainframe Operations

The integration of advanced technologies like AI and sophisticated data analysis tools in mainframe operations has led to innovative solutions that enhance performance, inform strategic decisions, and improve user experiences.

AI for Predictive Maintenance

1. **Case in Telecom Sector:** A telecommunications company integrated AI-driven predictive maintenance into its mainframe system. The AI algorithms analyzed system data to predict hardware failures and software performance issues. This approach allowed for maintenance to be scheduled proactively, reducing system downtime by 40%.
2. **Utility Company's Implementation:** A utility company employed AI to monitor its mainframe systems, crucial for managing grid operations. The AI predicted potential system overloads and suggested re-distribution of computational tasks, effectively preventing operational disruptions.

Data Analysis for Strategic Decisions

1. **Financial Institution Case Study:** A financial institution used automated data analysis tools for strategic decision-making. The system analyzed transaction data and user interactions, providing insights that led to a 30% reduction in processing resources during off-peak hours without affecting customer service quality.
2. **Retail Chain Optimization:** A retail chain utilized data analysis from its mainframe operations to optimize inventory management across its network. The insights helped in reallocating resources for peak shopping seasons,

enhancing supply chain efficiency.

Enhanced User Experience

1. **Healthcare Sector:** A hospital's mainframe system, equipped with automated workload management tools, improved patient data processing times. Faster access to medical records and test results enhanced the overall patient and healthcare provider experience.
2. **Online Education Platform:** An online education platform implemented an automated system to balance user loads during high-demand periods, like examinations or course enrollment phases. This led to reduced system response times and a more seamless experience for students and educators.

These examples showcase the transformative impact of innovative automation solutions in mainframe environments. The use of AI for predictive maintenance, data analysis for strategic decision-making, and automation for enhancing user experiences are pioneering steps towards more efficient, proactive, and user-centric mainframe operations.

Chapter 8. Scaling and Maintaining Automated Mainframe Systems

The effective scaling and maintenance of automated mainframe systems are vital for ensuring their long-term health and adaptability to changing business needs. This chapter delves into the challenges associated with scaling these systems, outlines maintenance strategies, and discusses approaches to ensure their long-term health.

8.1. Scalability Challenges and Solutions

Scalability Challenges

- **Handling Increased Workloads:** One of the primary challenges is ensuring the mainframe can handle increased workloads without performance degradation.
- **Integration with New Technologies:** As technology evolves, ensuring seamless integration without disrupting existing operations is a challenge.
- **Cost-Effective Scaling:** Balancing the need for increased capacity with cost constraints is often a major concern.

Solutions

- **Automated Resource Allocation:** Implementing

automated systems for dynamic resource allocation can help mainframes efficiently handle increased workloads.

- **Modular System Design:** Adopting a modular design allows for easier integration of new technologies and scaling of existing resources.
- **Cloud Integration:** Leveraging cloud environments can offer scalable solutions for storage and processing, providing flexibility and cost efficiency.

8.2. Maintenance Strategies for Automated Systems

Preventive Maintenance

- **Routine Checks:** Regularly scheduled checks and maintenance activities can prevent unexpected failures.
- **Software Updates:** Keeping all software, including automation tools, updated is key to preventing security vulnerabilities and compatibility issues.

Predictive Maintenance

- **Using Data Analytics:** Implementing data analytics to predict when parts of the system might fail allows for maintenance to be conducted before issues occur.
- **AI-Driven Insights:** AI can provide deeper insights into system performance, predicting potential failures based on historical and real-time data.

8.3. Ensuring Long-term System Health

Continuous Monitoring

- **Health Dashboards:** Implementing dashboards that provide real-time insights into system health is crucial for ongoing monitoring.

- **Automated Alerts:** Setting up automated alerts for any irregularities can help in quickly addressing potential issues.

Lifecycle Management

- **Regular Assessments:** Conducting regular assessments of the system's lifecycle can help in planning upgrades or replacements before performance is impacted.
- **Staying Current:** Keeping abreast of technological advancements and integrating them into the mainframe environment helps in maintaining the system's relevance and efficiency.

Training and Skills Development

- **Staff Training:** Regularly training staff on the latest mainframe technologies and best practices is essential for effective maintenance.
- **Knowledge Sharing:** Encouraging a culture of knowledge sharing and continuous learning can help in better managing and maintaining these complex systems.

Scaling and maintaining automated mainframe systems require a strategic approach, balancing the need for growth and innovation with the imperatives of system health and cost management. These strategies are critical for ensuring that mainframes continue to serve as reliable and efficient backbones for organizational IT infrastructures.

8.1. Scalability Challenges and Solutions

Scalability Challenges

Handling Increased Workloads

- **Performance Management:** The main challenge lies in scaling mainframe capacity to accommodate growing workloads without compromising performance. As demands increase, the system must continue to operate efficiently.

Integration with New Technologies

- **Seamless Integration:** Integrating evolving technologies with legacy mainframe systems without disrupting existing operations is a complex task. Compatibility and smooth integration are key concerns.

Cost-Effective Scaling

- **Budget Constraints:** Organizations must scale their mainframe operations cost-effectively. This involves making decisions about investments in hardware, software, and infrastructure that align with budget constraints and ROI considerations.

Solutions

Automated Resource Allocation

- **Dynamic Adjustment:** Automated systems can dynamically adjust resource allocation (like CPU, memory, storage) based on workload demands. This ensures optimal utilization of resources, enhancing performance during peak loads.

Modular System Design

- **Flexibility and Adaptability:** A modular approach to system design allows for the easier integration of new modules or technologies into the existing mainframe setup. This design makes scaling up or down more manageable and less disruptive.

Cloud Integration

- **Extended Capabilities:** Integrating cloud solutions can extend the capabilities of mainframe systems, particularly in terms of storage and processing power. Cloud environments offer scalable options that can be adjusted as per the changing needs of the organization.
- **Cost-Effective Scaling:** Leveraging cloud services can be more cost-effective than traditional scaling methods. It offers flexibility in terms of pay-as-you-go models, reducing upfront investments and allowing for better budget management.

Addressing scalability challenges in mainframe systems is critical to ensuring their longevity and effectiveness in handling evolving business needs. The strategic application of automated resource allocation, modular design, and cloud integration offers practical solutions to these challenges.

Scalability Challenges
Handling Increased Workloads
Performance Management

- Capacity Enhancement: The challenge lies in enhancing the mainframe's capacity to manage increased workloads without hindering its performance. This requires strategic planning to ensure that the system's throughput and efficiency do not decline as demands rise.
- Efficient Resource Allocation: Key to this challenge is the efficient allocation and utilization of resources such as processing power, memory, and storage to meet the growing needs without overburdening the system.

Integration with New Technologies
Seamless Integration

- Compatibility Issues: One of the significant challenges is integrating new, often more advanced technologies with existing legacy mainframe systems. Ensuring compatibility and maintaining seamless operations during this integration is complex.
- Minimizing Disruption: The integration process must minimize disruption to ongoing operations. This involves careful planning and testing to ensure new technologies work harmoniously with the existing mainframe architecture.

Cost-Effective Scaling
Budget Constraints

- Balancing Cost and Need: Organizations face the

challenge of scaling their mainframe operations in a way that is both effective and economically viable. Decisions regarding hardware upgrades, software enhancements, and infrastructure expansion need to be balanced with budgetary constraints.

- ROI Analysis: It's crucial to conduct a thorough return on investment (ROI) analysis when considering scaling options. This analysis should consider not just the immediate costs but also the long-term benefits and savings associated with the scaling efforts.
- Exploring Alternative Solutions: Often, cost-effective scaling may involve exploring alternative solutions like cloud integration or virtualization, which might offer more flexibility and scalability at a lower cost than traditional mainframe expansion methods.

Addressing these scalability challenges requires a multifaceted approach, combining strategic resource management, careful integration of new technologies, and a keen eye on cost-effectiveness. Successful navigation of these challenges ensures that mainframe systems remain robust, adaptable, and aligned with organizational growth and technological advancements.

Solutions to Scalability Challenges

Automated Resource Allocation

Dynamic Adjustment

- **Real-Time Resource Management:** Automated systems equipped with real-time monitoring can dynamically adjust the allocation of resources like CPU, memory, and storage. This responsiveness is critical in handling fluctuating workload demands.
- **Enhancing Performance During Peak Loads:** By automatically reallocating resources during peak demand periods, the system can maintain optimal performance levels, ensuring that processing power and memory are available where and when they are needed most.

Modular System Design

Flexibility and Adaptability

- **Ease of Integration:** A modular design approach in mainframe systems facilitates the integration of new modules or technologies. This strategy allows for incremental upgrades, thereby avoiding the need for large-scale overhauls.
- **Simplifying Scaling:** The modular approach simplifies both scaling up and scaling down processes. It allows for targeted enhancements or reductions in capacity, making the system more adaptable to changing business requirements.

Cloud Integration

Extended Capabilities

- **Enhanced Storage and Processing:** Integrating cloud solutions can significantly enhance the storage and processing capabilities of mainframe systems. Cloud platforms can provide additional processing power and storage space, accessible on demand.
- **Scalability and Flexibility:** The integration with cloud environments introduces a high degree of scalability and flexibility. This is particularly useful for handling workload spikes or for storing large volumes of data without the need for physical infrastructure expansion.

Cost-Effective Scaling

- **Reduced Upfront Investment:** Cloud services often operate on a pay-as-you-go model, which can be more cost-effective than traditional methods of scaling mainframe systems. This approach reduces the need for significant upfront capital investment.
- **Budget Management:** The cloud model allows for more predictable budgeting, with costs closely aligned to usage. This makes it easier for organizations to manage their budgets and reduces the financial risks associated with scaling mainframe operations.

Implementing these solutions — automated resource allocation, modular system design, and cloud integration — addresses the core challenges of scalability in mainframe systems. These strategies ensure that mainframes can efficiently and cost-effectively adapt to evolving business needs and technological advancements.

8.2. Maintenance Strategies for Automated Systems

Effective maintenance strategies are crucial for the long-term health and efficiency of automated mainframe systems. These strategies include both preventive and predictive maintenance approaches.

Preventive Maintenance

Routine Checks

- **Scheduled Maintenance Activities:** Regularly scheduled maintenance activities are essential for ensuring the system operates smoothly. This includes checking hardware components, reviewing software performance, and verifying the effectiveness of security measures.
- **Proactive Issue Identification:** Routine checks help in identifying potential issues before they escalate into major problems, reducing the likelihood of unexpected system failures.

Software Updates

- **Regular Updates:** Keeping all software, including operating systems, application software, and automation tools, updated is vital. Regular updates ensure that the system is protected against the latest security threats and runs on the most efficient and compatible software versions.

- **Patch Management:** Effective patch management is a key component of preventive maintenance. It involves timely application of software patches to address security vulnerabilities and functionality issues.

Predictive Maintenance

Using Data Analytics

- **Predictive System Health Checks:** By implementing data analytics, maintenance activities can be scheduled based on predictive insights. This approach uses system performance data to anticipate when parts of the system are likely to fail or require servicing.
- **Optimizing Maintenance Schedules:** Data analytics helps in creating optimized maintenance schedules that minimize downtime and are aligned with the system's usage patterns and historical performance data.

AI-Driven Insights

- **Advanced Predictive Capabilities:** AI algorithms can analyze complex patterns in system data to predict potential failures. This includes anticipating hardware malfunctions, software crashes, or network issues.
- **Historical and Real-Time Data Analysis:** AI-driven maintenance systems analyze both historical and real-time performance data. This comprehensive analysis provides a deeper understanding of the system's health and potential

future issues.

- **Automated Alerts and Recommendations:** AI systems can generate automated alerts about impending system issues and provide recommendations for preventive actions. This assists maintenance teams in prioritizing and addressing the most critical maintenance tasks.

Implementing a combination of preventive and predictive maintenance strategies is crucial for maintaining the health and efficiency of automated mainframe systems. These approaches help in minimizing downtime, enhancing system performance, and ensuring that the mainframe can reliably support the organization's operations.

Preventive Maintenance

Effective preventive maintenance is crucial for the smooth operation of automated mainframe systems. It involves routine checks and regular software updates to ensure system stability and security.

Routine Checks

Scheduled Maintenance Activities

- **Comprehensive System Review:** Regularly scheduled maintenance activities should encompass a thorough review of the mainframe's hardware components, software performance, and security protocols.
- **Hardware Inspection:** This includes inspecting physical components for signs of wear and tear, testing hardware functionality, and ensuring all components are operating within their specified parameters.
- **Software Assessment:** Software performance reviews involve checking system software, databases, and application performance to ensure they are running optimally.

Proactive Issue Identification

- **Early Detection:** Routine maintenance checks are critical for the early detection of potential issues, allowing for proactive intervention before these issues develop into significant problems.
- **System Health Indicators:** Monitoring key system health indicators such as processing speed, memory usage, and error logs can help identify emerging issues.

Software Updates

Regular Updates

- **Software Maintenance:** Keeping all software elements of the mainframe, including the operating system, application software, and automation tools, up-to-date is essential for the system's health.
- **Security and Efficiency:** Regular updates ensure the system is secured against the latest cyber threats and is operating on the most efficient and compatible versions of the software.

Patch Management

- **Timely Application:** Effective patch management involves the timely application of patches to the system's software. This is a critical aspect of maintaining software security and functionality.
- **Vulnerability Management:** Regular patching addresses known security vulnerabilities, reducing the risk of cyber attacks and system breaches.
- **Patch Testing:** Before applying patches, it's important to test them in a controlled environment to ensure they do not introduce new issues into the mainframe system.

Preventive maintenance, encompassing both routine checks and regular software updates, is a key strategy in maintaining the performance, security, and longevity of automated mainframe systems. This proactive approach helps in ensuring that these critical systems continue to function effectively and reliably.

Predictive Maintenance

Predictive maintenance utilizes advanced technologies like data analytics and AI to foresee potential system issues, enabling proactive maintenance actions. This approach is critical in minimizing downtime and extending the lifespan of mainframe systems.

Using Data Analytics

Predictive System Health Checks

- **Data-Driven Predictions:** Implementing data analytics allows for predictive system health checks. By analyzing performance data, the system can forecast when parts might fail or require maintenance.
- **Anticipating Failures:** This predictive approach uses system performance data to identify patterns that typically precede failures, allowing for intervention before issues become critical.

Optimizing Maintenance Schedules

- **Efficient Scheduling:** Data analytics assists in creating maintenance schedules that are both effective and minimally disruptive. These schedules are tailored to the system's usage patterns and historical performance data.
- **Reducing Downtime:** By optimizing maintenance schedules, the system can undergo necessary upkeep during periods of low activity, thereby minimizing the impact on operational efficiency.

AI-Driven Insights

Advanced Predictive Capabilities

- **Complex Pattern Analysis:** AI algorithms can analyze complex data patterns within the mainframe system to predict potential failures. This predictive capability can foresee a range of issues, from hardware malfunctions to software crashes or network problems.
- **Proactive System Care:** Anticipating these issues allows for proactive system care, addressing problems before they result in system downtime or major failures.

Historical and Real-Time Data Analysis

- **Comprehensive System Analysis:** AI-driven maintenance systems utilize both historical and real-time data to provide a comprehensive view of the system's health. This dual analysis offers a more complete understanding of the system's operational state.
- **Deeper Insights:** Analyzing historical data helps in identifying long-term trends and degradation patterns, while real-time data offers immediate insights into the system's current performance.

Automated Alerts and Recommendations

- **Intelligent Alert System:** AI systems can generate automated alerts when they detect indicators of potential system issues. These alerts enable maintenance teams to respond promptly to emerging problems.
- **Actionable Recommendations:** Along with alerts, AI systems can also provide recommendations for preventive actions. These suggestions help maintenance teams in efficiently prioritizing and addressing maintenance tasks.

Predictive maintenance, empowered by data analytics and AI, represents a significant advancement in mainframe system care. It shifts the maintenance approach from reactive to proactive, ensuring that the mainframe systems are not only maintained effectively but also optimized for future performance and reliability.

8.3. Ensuring Long-term System Health

Maintaining the long-term health of automated mainframe systems is essential for ensuring their reliability and efficiency over time. This involves continuous monitoring, lifecycle management, and ongoing training and skills development.

Continuous Monitoring

Health Dashboards

- **Real-Time System Insights:** Implementing health dashboards provides real-time insights into various aspects of system health, such as performance metrics, resource utilization, and operational status.
- **Proactive Health Management:** These dashboards enable IT teams to proactively manage the system's health, identifying and addressing issues as they arise.

Automated Alerts

- **Immediate Notification:** Setting up automated alerts for any irregularities in system performance or behavior ensures that potential issues are quickly brought to the attention of the maintenance team.
- **Prompt Issue Resolution:** Automated alerts facilitate

prompt responses to system irregularities, minimizing the impact on system performance and preventing minor issues from escalating.

Lifecycle Management
Regular Assessments

- **System Health Evaluations:** Conducting regular assessments of the mainframe's lifecycle helps in understanding its current state and predicting future performance.
- **Proactive Upgrade Planning:** These assessments are crucial for planning upgrades or replacements before the system's performance is significantly impacted, ensuring continuous system efficiency.

Staying Current

- **Technological Advancements:** Keeping abreast of the latest technological advancements and integrating them into the mainframe environment is key to maintaining the system's relevance and operational efficiency.
- **Adaptation to Changing Needs:** Regularly updating the system with new technologies ensures it remains capable of meeting evolving business demands.

Training and Skills Development
Staff Training

- **Skill Enhancement:** Regular training sessions for staff on the latest mainframe technologies and best practices are essential. This training ensures that the team is well-equipped to manage and maintain the system effectively.

- **Adapting to New Technologies:** As new technologies are integrated into the mainframe environment, it's important that staff are trained to work with these advancements efficiently.

Knowledge Sharing

- **Collaborative Learning Environment:** Encouraging a culture of knowledge sharing and continuous learning within the organization helps in creating a more informed and skilled maintenance team.
- **Best Practices and Experience Sharing:** Facilitating forums for sharing best practices and experiences can lead to more effective management and maintenance of these complex systems.

Ensuring the long-term health of automated mainframe systems is a comprehensive process that involves vigilant monitoring, proactive lifecycle management, and continuous staff training and development. These practices are essential for maintaining the system's efficiency, reliability, and relevance in a rapidly evolving technological landscape.

Chapter 9. Future Trends in Mainframe Automation

As we look ahead, the landscape of mainframe automation is poised to evolve rapidly, driven by emerging technologies and innovative approaches. This chapter explores these upcoming trends, offering insights into the future of mainframe automation and preparing for the next wave of technological advancements.

9.1. Emerging Technologies and Their Impact

Integration of Advanced AI and Machine Learning

- **Enhanced Decision-Making:** The integration of AI and machine learning into mainframe systems will bring about smarter decision-making capabilities, allowing for more sophisticated data processing and analysis.
- **Automated Problem Solving:** These technologies can help automate complex problem-solving processes, leading to quicker and more efficient resolution of system issues.

Adoption of Blockchain Technology

- **Enhanced Security and Transparency:** The adoption of blockchain technology in mainframe environments could revolutionize data security and integrity, providing a new level of transparency in data transactions.

Quantum Computing

- **Processing Power Revolution:** Quantum computing presents the potential to dramatically increase the processing power available to mainframes, enabling them to handle tasks that are currently impossible or impractical.

9.2. Predictions for the Future of Mainframe Automation Growth in Cloud Integration

- **Hybrid Models:** There will likely be a continued trend towards hybrid cloud-mainframe models, offering the best of both worlds – mainframe reliability with cloud scalability and innovation.

Enhanced Cybersecurity Measures

- **Proactive Security:** As cybersecurity threats evolve, mainframe systems will increasingly incorporate proactive security measures, utilizing predictive analytics to prevent attacks before they occur.

More User-Friendly Interfaces

- **Enhanced Accessibility:** We can expect to see more user-friendly interfaces for managing mainframe systems, making them more accessible to a broader range of users and administrators.

9.3. Preparing for the Next Wave of Innovations Investing in Skills and Training

- **Keeping Up with Changes:** As technologies evolve, investing in ongoing training and skill development for IT staff will be crucial to keep up with the latest trends and make the most of new mainframe capabilities.

Flexible and Adaptive IT Strategies

- **Embracing Change:** Organizations should develop flexible and adaptive IT strategies that allow them to quickly adopt and integrate new technologies as they emerge.

Collaboration with Technology Partners

- **Staying Ahead:** Collaborating with technology partners and vendors will be key in staying ahead of the curve. These partnerships can provide insights into emerging trends and access to the latest technologies.

The future of mainframe automation is an exciting frontier, marked by advancements in AI, cloud computing, and cybersecurity. Staying informed and adaptable will be key for organizations looking to leverage these new technologies to enhance their mainframe systems.

9.1. Emerging Technologies and Their Impact

The mainframe computing landscape is on the brink of significant changes, driven by the emergence of cutting-edge technologies. These advancements promise to enhance decision-making capabilities, revolutionize security, and exponentially increase processing power.

Integration of Advanced AI and Machine Learning

Enhanced Decision-Making

- **Data-Driven Insights:** AI and machine learning integration will enable mainframe systems to process and analyze vast amounts of data more efficiently, leading to more informed and accurate decision-making.
- **Predictive Analytics:** These technologies will allow for predictive analytics, enabling businesses to anticipate trends, customer behavior, and potential system issues before they occur.

Automated Problem Solving

- **Efficient Issue Resolution:** AI and machine learning can automate the resolution of complex system issues, reducing the time and effort required for problem-solving.

- **Self-Optimizing Systems:** Mainframes will become increasingly self-optimizing, automatically adjusting their operations to optimize performance and efficiency.

Adoption of Blockchain Technology
Enhanced Security and Transparency

- **Data Integrity:** Blockchain's decentralized and immutable ledger system could significantly enhance data security and integrity in mainframe environments.
- **Transaction Verification:** Its application could be particularly transformative in sectors like finance and healthcare, where secure and transparent transaction verification is paramount.

Quantum Computing
Processing Power Revolution

- **Handling Complex Computations:** The advent of quantum computing holds the promise of providing unprecedented levels of processing power, enabling mainframes to handle highly complex computations that are beyond the reach of classical computing.
- **Solving Intractable Problems:** Quantum computing could be pivotal in solving complex scientific, encryption, and data analysis problems that are currently intractable.

These emerging technologies are set to redefine the capabilities of mainframe systems, making them more powerful, secure, and intelligent. The integration of AI and machine learning, the adoption of blockchain technology, and the advent of quantum computing are not just incremental upgrades but are poised to trigger a paradigm shift in mainframe computing.

Integration of Advanced AI and Machine Learning

The integration of AI and machine learning into mainframe systems marks a significant leap forward in automation, offering enhanced capabilities in decision-making and problem-solving.

Enhanced Decision-Making

Data-Driven Insights

- **Efficient Data Processing:** With AI and machine learning, mainframe systems will be able to process and analyze large datasets more efficiently, extracting valuable insights that were previously unattainable due to the sheer volume and complexity of the data.
- **Informed Decision-Making:** This capability will enable more informed and accurate decision-making processes, as organizations will have access to deeper and more nuanced understandings of their data.

Predictive Analytics

- **Anticipating Future Trends:** AI and machine learning enable predictive analytics, which can foresee trends, customer behaviors, and potential system issues before they manifest.
- **Proactive Business Strategies:** By anticipating these trends and behaviors, businesses can develop more proactive and strategic approaches, positioning themselves advantageously in their respective markets.

Automated Problem Solving

Efficient Issue Resolution

- **Automating Complex Tasks:** AI and machine learning

can greatly reduce the time and effort required to resolve complex system issues. This includes automating tasks such as diagnosing system problems, identifying inefficiencies, or optimizing workflows.

- **Reduced Downtime:** The ability to quickly and efficiently resolve issues means reduced downtime for mainframe systems, ensuring continuous and smooth operations.

Self-Optimizing Systems

- **Adaptive Operations:** Mainframes will evolve to become increasingly self-optimizing. Leveraging AI and machine learning, these systems will be capable of automatically adjusting their operations in response to changing conditions and requirements.
- **Maximizing Efficiency and Performance:** This self-optimization will ensure that mainframe systems operate at peak efficiency, adjusting resource allocation and operational parameters to optimize performance continuously.

The integration of advanced AI and machine learning into mainframe automation represents a transformative shift, making these systems more intelligent, responsive, and efficient. As these technologies continue to evolve, they will play a pivotal role in shaping the future of mainframe computing.

Adoption of Blockchain Technology

The incorporation of blockchain technology into mainframe systems is poised to revolutionize how data security and transaction verification are handled, especially in industries where these aspects are critical.

Enhanced Security and Transparency

Data Integrity

- **Decentralized and Immutable Records:** Blockchain technology introduces a decentralized ledger system for mainframes, where data is stored in an immutable manner. This means that once a piece of data is entered into the blockchain, it cannot be altered or deleted, significantly enhancing data integrity and security.
- **Protection Against Tampering:** The inherent security features of blockchain, such as cryptographic hashing and consensus algorithms, make it incredibly difficult for data to be tampered with. This is especially beneficial for mainframe environments that handle sensitive or critical data.

Transaction Verification

- **Secure Transactions in Finance:** In the financial sector, blockchain can transform how transactions are recorded and verified. The technology's ability to provide a secure and unalterable record of transactions makes it ideal for applications like fund transfers, settlements, and compliance tracking.
- **Transparency in Healthcare:** In healthcare, blockchain technology can ensure the integrity and verifiability of patient records, treatment histories, and pharmaceutical

transactions. This transparency is crucial for patient safety, privacy, and compliance with regulatory standards.

- **Audit Trails:** The adoption of blockchain in mainframes would create transparent and verifiable audit trails, enhancing trust and accountability in processes that are critical to finance and healthcare sectors.

The adoption of blockchain technology in mainframe automation opens up new possibilities for enhancing data security and providing transparent transaction verification. Its impact could be particularly transformative in sectors where data integrity and security are of utmost importance, heralding a new era of trust and transparency in digital transactions.

Quantum Computing

The integration of quantum computing into mainframe environments represents a significant advancement, potentially revolutionizing the processing capabilities and solving capabilities of these systems.

Processing Power Revolution

Handling Complex Computations

- **Enhanced Processing Capabilities:** Quantum computing offers a quantum leap in processing power. This advanced technology operates on principles of quantum mechanics, enabling it to perform complex computations at speeds unattainable by traditional computing methods.
- **Expanding Mainframe Capabilities:** With quantum computing, mainframes could handle calculations involving large datasets, complex algorithms, and simulations much more efficiently. This advancement would significantly broaden the scope of problems mainframes can tackle, especially in data-heavy fields like big data analytics and artificial intelligence.

Solving Intractable Problems

- **Breaking Computational Barriers:** Quantum computing has the potential to solve problems that are currently considered intractable for classical computers. This includes complex optimization problems, simulations of molecular and chemical interactions, and advanced cryptographic algorithms.
- **Revolutionizing Scientific Research:** In scientific research, quantum computing could accelerate discoveries by enabling the analysis of massively complex datasets and

the simulation of physical processes at a quantum level.

- **Advancing Cryptography and Security:** The field of cryptography will see a significant impact. Quantum computing could potentially crack complex encryption methods used today, necessitating the development of quantum-resistant cryptographic techniques.

The advent of quantum computing in the realm of mainframe automation could usher in a new era of computational capabilities, allowing for the processing of previously unsolvable problems and vastly enhancing the speed and efficiency of complex computations. As this technology continues to develop, it is poised to drastically change the landscape of computational problem-solving and data processing.

9.2. Predictions for the Future of Mainframe Automation

The future of mainframe automation is marked by several key trends, each aimed at enhancing efficiency, security, and accessibility. These trends indicate a shift towards more integrated, proactive, and user-centric mainframe systems.

Growth in Cloud Integration

Hybrid Models

- **Combining Strengths:** The trend towards hybrid cloud-mainframe models is expected to grow, combining the reliability and robust processing power of mainframes with the scalability and innovative capabilities of cloud computing.
- **Flexibility and Efficiency:** Such models will provide organizations with greater flexibility in managing workloads, allowing them to leverage cloud resources for variable demands while relying on mainframes for core, high-volume processing tasks.
- **Cost-Effectiveness:** Hybrid models can also offer a more cost-effective solution, optimizing resource utilization and reducing the need for large-scale physical infrastructure

investments.

Enhanced Cybersecurity Measures
Proactive Security

- **Anticipatory Defense:** As cybersecurity threats become more sophisticated, mainframe systems are likely to adopt more proactive security measures. This could include advanced threat detection systems that utilize machine learning and AI for predictive analytics, identifying and mitigating potential threats before they materialize.
- **Continuous Monitoring:** Enhanced security measures will likely involve continuous monitoring of system activities, with automated responses to detected anomalies to protect sensitive data and system integrity.

More User-Friendly Interfaces
Enhanced Accessibility

- **Simplifying Management:** The future of mainframe automation will likely see the development of more user-friendly interfaces. These interfaces will aim to simplify the management and operation of mainframe systems, making them more accessible to a broader range of users and administrators.
- **Improving Usability:** Enhanced interfaces will focus on improving usability, including more intuitive navigation, visualization tools, and simplified control mechanisms. This will make it easier for non-specialist staff to manage and interact with mainframe systems.
- **Integration with Modern Tools:** Expect these interfaces to integrate more seamlessly with modern tools and

platforms, offering a more unified and coherent user experience across various IT environments.

These predictions for the future of mainframe automation highlight a trajectory towards greater integration, enhanced security, and improved user experience. By embracing these trends, mainframe systems will continue to evolve, remaining vital and relevant in the ever-changing landscape of information technology.

Growth in Cloud Integration

Hybrid Models

Combining Strengths

- **Leveraging Mainframe and Cloud Advantages:** The growing trend towards hybrid cloud-mainframe models is a response to the need for both the power and reliability of traditional mainframes and the agility and innovation offered by cloud computing.
- **Optimized Performance:** In these models, mainframes continue to handle high-volume, mission-critical tasks while cloud platforms are used for their scalability and capacity to innovate, resulting in a system that leverages the strengths of both technologies.

Flexibility and Efficiency

- **Dynamic Workload Management:** Hybrid models provide significant flexibility in workload management. Organizations can dynamically shift less critical or variable workloads to the cloud, reserving mainframe capacity for essential processing tasks.
- **Responsive to Business Needs:** This flexibility ensures that computing resources are aligned more closely with business needs, allowing for rapid scaling in response to demand fluctuations.

Cost-Effectiveness

- **Reducing Infrastructure Costs:** By adopting a hybrid model, organizations can avoid the high costs associated with expanding physical mainframe infrastructure. Cloud services typically offer pay-as-you-go models, which can be more economical.

- **Optimized Resource Utilization:** Hybrid models enable organizations to optimize their resource utilization, ensuring they are not paying for idle mainframe capacity during periods of low demand. This can lead to significant cost savings and more efficient overall resource management.

The trend towards integrating cloud computing with traditional mainframe systems signifies a strategic shift in enterprise computing. This hybrid approach promises enhanced flexibility, efficiency, and cost-effectiveness, ensuring that organizations can meet both their current and future computing needs while maximizing the return on their technology investments.

Enhanced Cybersecurity Measures

The escalation of cybersecurity threats necessitates a more proactive and sophisticated approach to security in mainframe systems. Future trends point towards leveraging advanced technologies to anticipate and counteract these threats effectively.

Proactive Security

Anticipatory Defense

- **Predictive Threat Identification:** With the increasing sophistication of cyber threats, mainframe systems are expected to adopt advanced threat detection systems. These systems, powered by AI and machine learning, will employ predictive analytics to identify potential threats before they materialize, allowing for preemptive defensive actions.
- **Adaptive Security Posture:** The integration of AI in cybersecurity will enable mainframes to adapt their security posture based on evolving threat landscapes. This includes updating security protocols automatically in response to detected threats and vulnerabilities.

Continuous Monitoring

- **Real-Time Surveillance:** Future mainframe security measures are likely to involve continuous, real-time monitoring of all system activities. This comprehensive surveillance will ensure that any unusual or suspicious behavior is detected as it occurs.
- **Automated Response Mechanisms:** Upon detecting anomalies, these systems will be capable of initiating automated responses. These could range from simple alerts to more complex actions like isolating affected network

segments or initiating countermeasures against ongoing attacks.

- **Protecting Data Integrity:** Continuous monitoring will play a crucial role in protecting the integrity and confidentiality of sensitive data. By detecting and responding to threats in real-time, mainframes can safeguard critical information more effectively.

Enhanced cybersecurity measures, especially those incorporating proactive defense strategies and continuous monitoring, are pivotal for the future of mainframe automation. These advanced security protocols will not only defend against current threats but also adapt to counter future, more sophisticated cyber attacks, ensuring the security and reliability of mainframe systems in an increasingly digital world.

More User-Friendly Interfaces

The evolution of mainframe interfaces towards greater user-friendliness and accessibility is a key trend in the future of mainframe automation. This shift is aimed at simplifying the complexity traditionally associated with mainframe systems, making them more accessible and easier to manage.

Enhanced Accessibility

Simplifying Management

- **Broadening User Base:** Future developments in mainframe interfaces are expected to simplify the management and operation of these systems. This approach aims to make mainframes more accessible, not just to experienced technicians but also to a broader range of users and administrators.
- **Reducing Complexity:** By simplifying the interface, organizations can reduce the complexity often associated with mainframe management, making it easier for users to perform essential tasks without extensive specialized training.

Improving Usability

- **Intuitive User Experience:** Enhanced interfaces will likely emphasize usability, featuring more intuitive navigation, clear and simple visualizations, and user-friendly control mechanisms.
- **Empowering Non-Specialists:** These improvements in usability are crucial for enabling non-specialist staff to effectively manage and interact with mainframe systems, thereby democratizing access to this powerful technology.

Integration with Modern Tools

- **Seamless Integration:** Future mainframe interfaces are expected to integrate more seamlessly with modern tools and platforms. This integration is key to offering a unified user experience across various IT environments.
- **Consistent User Experience:** The aim is to provide a consistent and coherent experience, whether users are working within the mainframe environment or utilizing other IT tools and platforms. This consistency will help in minimizing the learning curve and improving overall efficiency.
- **Adaptation to New Technologies:** As mainframe systems continue to evolve and incorporate new technologies, their interfaces will also need to adapt, ensuring that users can leverage the full range of functionalities offered by these advanced systems.

The development of more user-friendly interfaces for mainframe systems represents a significant step towards making this powerful technology more accessible and easier to use. By focusing on simplifying management, improving usability, and integrating with modern tools, the future of mainframe automation looks poised to break down traditional barriers, opening up these systems to a wider range of users.

9.3. Preparing for the Next Wave of Innovations

As mainframe automation continues to evolve rapidly, organizations need to prepare strategically to harness these advancements effectively. This preparation involves investing in workforce capabilities, adopting flexible IT strategies, and fostering strong collaborations with technology partners.

Investing in Skills and Training

Keeping Up with Changes

- **Continuous Learning:** As new technologies transform mainframe automation, ongoing training and skill development for IT staff become crucial. This ensures that the workforce is equipped to handle and make the most of the latest mainframe capabilities.
- **Specialized Training Programs:** Implementing specialized training programs focusing on emerging technologies like AI, machine learning, and cloud integration will be key. Such programs should be designed to keep pace with technological advancements and industry trends.

Flexible and Adaptive IT Strategies

Embracing Change

- **Agile IT Frameworks:** Organizations should develop flexible and adaptive IT strategies that enable them to swiftly adopt and integrate emerging technologies. This agility will allow them to capitalize on new opportunities and respond to challenges effectively.
- **Scalability and Adaptability:** Strategies should emphasize scalability and adaptability, ensuring that IT infrastructures, including mainframe systems, can adjust to changing business needs and technological landscapes without extensive overhauls.

Collaboration with Technology Partners

Staying Ahead

- **Partnering for Innovation:** Collaborating with technology partners and vendors is essential to stay ahead in the rapidly evolving field of mainframe automation. These partnerships offer valuable insights into emerging trends and provide access to cutting-edge technologies.
- **Joint Development Initiatives:** Engaging in joint development initiatives with technology partners can lead to customized solutions that precisely meet organizational needs. It can also provide an opportunity for early adoption of innovative technologies.
- **Knowledge Exchange:** Collaborations can facilitate a two-way exchange of knowledge and expertise, benefiting both organizations and their technology partners. This exchange can drive innovation and lead to the development of more robust and effective mainframe

solutions.

Preparing for the next wave of innovations in mainframe automation requires a proactive approach focused on continuous learning, adaptable strategies, and collaborative partnerships. By embracing these elements, organizations can position themselves to effectively leverage new technologies and maintain a competitive edge in the digital era.

Investing in Skills and Training

To harness the full potential of rapidly advancing mainframe technologies, a strategic investment in skills and training is essential. This initiative is pivotal for empowering IT professionals to adapt to and efficiently manage the evolving landscape of mainframe automation.

Keeping Up with Changes

Continuous Learning

- **Adapting to Technological Evolution:** In an environment where technological advancements are constant, ongoing learning and skill development for IT staff are indispensable. This approach ensures that the workforce stays abreast of the latest developments in mainframe automation.
- **Customized Learning Pathways:** Continuous learning can be facilitated through customized training programs and learning pathways that focus on up-to-date skills and knowledge relevant to modern mainframe systems.

Specialized Training Programs

- **Focus on Emerging Technologies:** Given the rapid integration of technologies like AI, machine learning, and cloud computing into mainframe environments, specialized training programs in these areas are crucial. These programs should cover not only the technical aspects but also strategic applications of these technologies in mainframe contexts.
- **Alignment with Industry Trends:** Training initiatives need to be closely aligned with current industry trends and technological advancements. This ensures that the skills

developed are relevant and immediately applicable to contemporary mainframe environments.

- **Hands-On Experience:** Effective training programs should include practical, hands-on experience with new technologies. Simulations, lab exercises, and real-world project work can significantly enhance the learning experience, enabling IT staff to gain practical insights into the application of new technologies in their work environments.

Investing in skills and training is critical for organizations looking to capitalize on the advancements in mainframe automation. Continuous learning and specialized training programs tailored to emerging technologies will equip IT professionals with the necessary skills and knowledge to navigate and excel in this evolving field.

Flexible and Adaptive IT Strategies

In an era marked by rapid technological evolution, organizations need to adopt IT strategies that are not only robust but also flexible and adaptive. This approach is key to staying competitive and responsive in a fast-changing digital landscape.

Embracing Change

Agile IT Frameworks

- **Dynamic Approach to Technology Integration:** Developing agile IT frameworks is essential for organizations to swiftly adopt and integrate emerging technologies. This agility facilitates quick adaptation to new opportunities and effective response to emerging challenges.
- **Continuous Improvement Cycle:** Agile frameworks typically involve a continuous cycle of development, testing, and refinement, enabling organizations to innovate rapidly and iteratively. This approach is crucial in environments where technological changes are frequent and unpredictable.

Scalability and Adaptability

- **Responsive IT Infrastructures:** IT strategies should prioritize scalability and adaptability. This means designing infrastructures, including mainframe systems, that can easily scale up or down and adapt to changing business requirements and technological advancements.
- **Minimizing Overhaul Needs:** By focusing on scalability and adaptability, organizations can avoid the need for extensive overhauls when adapting to new technologies or scaling their operations. This not only saves time and

resources but also reduces operational disruptions.

- **Future-Proofing IT Systems:** A flexible and adaptive strategy helps in future-proofing IT systems. By anticipating future trends and building systems that can adapt to these trends, organizations can maintain a competitive edge and ensure long-term operational efficiency.

Adopting flexible and adaptive IT strategies is vital in a landscape where change is the only constant. By embracing agile frameworks and focusing on scalability and adaptability, organizations can ensure their IT infrastructures, especially mainframe systems, remain effective, efficient, and relevant in the face of continuous technological evolution.

Collaboration with Technology Partners

In the rapidly advancing domain of mainframe automation, maintaining a competitive edge requires not just internal innovation, but also active collaboration with external technology partners and vendors. These collaborations are instrumental in staying current with emerging trends and accessing novel technologies.

Staying Ahead

Partnering for Innovation

- **Access to New Technologies:** Collaborating with technology partners and vendors provides organizations with critical insights into emerging trends in mainframe automation. These partnerships are gateways to cutting-edge technologies, often offering early access to new tools and solutions.
- **Strategic Alignment:** Partnerships with technology innovators can help align an organization's IT strategy with the latest technological advancements, ensuring that mainframe systems are not only current but also forward-thinking.

Joint Development Initiatives

- **Tailored Solutions:** Engaging in joint development initiatives with technology partners allows for the creation of customized solutions that are closely aligned with an organization's specific needs and challenges. This collaborative development can result in more effective and efficient mainframe automation tools.
- **Early Adoption Benefits:** Such collaborations can also provide opportunities for early adoption of innovative technologies. Early adopters can gain a significant

competitive advantage by implementing the latest solutions before they become widely available.

Knowledge Exchange

- **Mutual Learning:** Collaborations with technology partners facilitate a two-way exchange of knowledge and expertise. This exchange is mutually beneficial, driving innovation and leading to the development of more robust and effective mainframe solutions.
- **Expanding Expertise:** Through these partnerships, organizations can tap into a broader pool of knowledge and experience, expanding their own expertise and understanding of mainframe automation. This can be particularly valuable in navigating the complexities of integrating new technologies with existing mainframe infrastructures.
- **Networking and Relationship Building:** Collaborative efforts also foster stronger relationships within the technology community, creating a network of support and knowledge that can be leveraged for future projects and innovation efforts.

Collaboration with technology partners is a strategic imperative in the evolving landscape of mainframe automation. By partnering for innovation, engaging in joint development initiatives, and facilitating knowledge exchange, organizations can ensure that their mainframe systems stay at the forefront of technological advancement, driving efficiency, competitiveness, and innovation.

Chapter 10. Case Studies and Real-World Applications

This chapter explores various case studies and real-world applications of mainframe automation, providing insights into successful implementations, lessons learned, and how innovations in automation are impacting different industries.

10.1. Success Stories in Mainframe Automation

Notable Achievements

- **Efficiency Improvements:** Case studies showcasing how automation has streamlined operations in organizations, leading to significant improvements in processing times and operational efficiency.
- **Cost Reductions:** Examples where automation has led to substantial cost savings, either through reduced labor costs, lower operational expenses, or more efficient use of resources.

Innovative Use Cases

- **Integration with Emerging Technologies:** Real-world examples of how integrating AI, machine learning, or cloud computing with mainframe systems has enhanced business capabilities.

- **Complex Problem-Solving:** Instances where mainframe automation has been utilized to solve complex business challenges, demonstrating the versatility and power of these systems.

10.2. Lessons Learned from Automation Projects

Key Insights

- **Best Practices:** Analysis of successful automation projects to extract best practices and strategies that can be applied in future initiatives.
- **Challenges and Solutions:** Discussions of challenges encountered during automation projects and how they were overcome, providing valuable learning points for similar future endeavors.

Risk Management and Planning

- **Strategic Planning:** Insights into the importance of strategic planning in automation projects, including resource allocation, timeline management, and stakeholder involvement.
- **Mitigating Risks:** Lessons learned in identifying and mitigating risks associated with mainframe automation projects.

10.3. Innovations in Different Industries

Sector-Specific Innovations

- **Finance and Banking:** Examples of how mainframe automation has revolutionized operations in the finance

sector, such as through automated transaction processing or fraud detection systems.
- **Healthcare:** Case studies illustrating the impact of mainframe automation in healthcare, including patient data management and research data analysis.

Emerging Trends

- **Retail and E-commerce:** Insights into how automation in mainframes is being used to manage vast transaction volumes and customer data in the retail sector.
- **Government and Public Sector:** Examples of mainframe automation in public services, highlighting efficiencies in data processing and public record management.

This chapter provides a comprehensive overview of the tangible impacts of mainframe automation across various sectors. By examining success stories, extracting lessons learned, and exploring sector-specific innovations, it offers a well-rounded perspective on the real-world implications and benefits of mainframe automation.

10.1. Success Stories in Mainframe Automation

This section delves into various success stories in the realm of mainframe automation, highlighting how organizations have leveraged automation to enhance efficiency, reduce costs, and solve complex problems.

Notable Achievements

Efficiency Improvements

- **Streamlined Banking Processes:** A leading bank implemented mainframe automation for its transaction processing system, resulting in a 40% reduction in processing times and significantly improved customer service efficiency.
- **Optimized Healthcare Data Management:** A healthcare provider utilized mainframe automation to streamline patient data processing, reducing the time for data retrieval by 30%, thereby enhancing patient care and operational efficiency.

Cost Reductions

- **Automated Retail Inventory Management:** A retail giant employed mainframe automation for inventory management, leading to a 25% reduction in operational costs through optimized stock handling and reduced labor requirements.

- **Energy Sector Efficiency:** An energy company integrated automation into its mainframe systems for monitoring and managing energy grids, achieving a 20% reduction in operational expenses through improved system management and reduced manual interventions.

Innovative Use Cases

Integration with Emerging Technologies

- **AI-Enhanced Financial Forecasting:** A financial institution integrated AI with its mainframe system for predictive analysis of market trends, resulting in more accurate financial forecasting and strategic investment decisions.
- **Cloud-Enabled Government Services:** A government agency adopted a cloud-integrated mainframe system, enhancing its ability to manage public records and services, offering more scalable and flexible public service delivery.

Complex Problem-Solving

- **Machine Learning in Logistics:** A logistics company used machine learning algorithms in its mainframe system to optimize delivery routes and schedules, solving complex logistical challenges and improving delivery times by 35%.
- **Advanced Analytics in Manufacturing:** A manufacturing firm implemented advanced data analytics in its mainframe system for predictive maintenance of machinery, significantly reducing downtime and maintenance costs.

These success stories in mainframe automation illustrate the transformative impact of automation technologies across various industries. From efficiency improvements and cost reductions to innovative uses of AI and machine learning, mainframe automation has proven to be a pivotal element in driving business growth and solving complex operational challenges.

Notable Achievements in Efficiency Improvements and Cost Reductions

Streamlined Banking Processes

- **Case Study: Major Banking Institution**
  - **Automation Implementation:** The bank integrated automation into its transaction processing system within its mainframe environment.
  - **Results:** Achieved a 40% reduction in transaction processing times, leading to quicker customer service and improved overall efficiency in banking operations.

Optimized Healthcare Data Management

- **Case Study: Healthcare Provider**
  - **Automation Application:** Utilized mainframe automation for more efficient patient data processing.
  - **Outcome:** Reduced time for patient data retrieval by 30%, enhancing patient care efficiency and streamlining operational processes in healthcare services.

Automated Retail Inventory Management

- **Case Study: Retail Industry Giant**
  - **Automation Strategy:** Implemented mainframe automation in inventory management systems.
  - **Impact:** Realized a 25% reduction in operational costs due to more optimized stock handling and reduced labor

requirements, leading to more efficient inventory control and cost savings.

Energy Sector Efficiency

- **Case Study: Energy Company**
  - **Integration of Automation:** Employed automation in mainframe systems for enhanced monitoring and management of energy grids.
  - **Efficiency Gains:** Achieved a 20% reduction in operational expenses, attributed to improved system management and significant reductions in manual interventions, thereby increasing operational efficiency in energy management.

These case studies across various industries demonstrate how mainframe automation has been a game-changer in enhancing operational efficiency and reducing costs. From banking and healthcare to retail and energy sectors, the strategic implementation of mainframe automation has led to significant improvements in processing times, customer service, inventory management, and operational expenses. These successes underscore the transformative impact of automation in modernizing and optimizing enterprise operations.

Innovative Use Cases in Integration with Emerging Technologies and Complex Problem-Solving

Integration with Emerging Technologies

1. **AI-Enhanced Financial Forecasting**
    - **Case Study: Financial Institution**
        - **Implementation:** Integrated AI for predictive analysis into its mainframe system.
        - **Outcome:** The integration led to more accurate forecasting of market trends, enabling the institution to make more strategic investment decisions. This significantly improved the accuracy of financial predictions and risk assessments.
2. **Cloud-Enabled Government Services**
    - **Case Study: Government Agency**
        - **Adoption Strategy:** Adopted a cloud-integrated mainframe system.
        - **Impact:** Enhanced the agency's ability to manage public records and services, resulting in more scalable and flexible public service delivery. This integration improved accessibility to public records and streamlined service processes.

Complex Problem-Solving

1. **Machine Learning in Logistics**
    - **Case Study: Logistics Company**
        - **Innovation:** Utilized machine learning algorithms in its mainframe system to optimize delivery routes and schedules.
        - **Results:** Successfully solved complex logistical challenges, leading to a 35% improvement in

delivery times and significant cost savings in fuel and labor.

2. **Advanced Analytics in Manufacturing**
    - **Case Study: Manufacturing Firm**
        - **Application:** Implemented advanced data analytics in its mainframe system for predictive maintenance.
        - **Benefits:** Achieved significant reductions in machinery downtime and maintenance costs. This proactive approach to maintenance led to enhanced operational efficiency and equipment longevity.

These innovative use cases illustrate how the integration of emerging technologies like AI, cloud computing, and machine learning with mainframe systems can lead to groundbreaking improvements in various industries. From enhanced financial forecasting and flexible government services to optimized logistics and predictive maintenance in manufacturing, these examples demonstrate the transformative power of combining mainframe robustness with advanced technological capabilities.

10.2. Lessons Learned from Automation Projects

The experience gained from past automation projects offers invaluable insights into best practices, challenges and solutions, risk management, and strategic planning. These lessons are crucial for guiding future automation endeavors.

Key Insights

Best Practices

- **Effective Communication:** One of the key best practices identified is the importance of effective communication throughout the automation project. This includes clear articulation of goals, regular updates, and stakeholder engagement.
- **Iterative Development:** Successful projects often adopt an iterative approach, allowing for continuous feedback and adjustment, which leads to better end results.

Challenges and Solutions

- **Integration Challenges:** Many projects face challenges in integrating new automation technologies with existing systems. Solutions include thorough testing and phased implementation strategies.

- **Skill Gaps:** Addressing skill gaps in teams is another common challenge. Solutions often involve targeted training programs and sometimes bringing in external expertise.

Risk Management and Planning

Strategic Planning

- **Clear Roadmap:** A key lesson is the importance of having a clear strategic roadmap for the automation project. This involves setting realistic goals, timelines, and measurable milestones.
- **Resource Allocation:** Effective allocation of resources, both human and technological, is essential. Planning should ensure that the necessary skills and technologies are available throughout the project.

Mitigating Risks

- **Risk Identification:** Early identification of potential risks is crucial. This can involve technical risks, such as compatibility issues, as well as operational risks like potential disruptions to business processes.
- **Contingency Planning:** Successful projects have robust contingency plans in place. This involves having fallback options and strategies to address unforeseen challenges that arise during the project.

Lessons learned from previous mainframe automation projects provide a rich source of knowledge for organizations embarking on similar endeavors. By understanding and applying these insights, businesses can avoid common pitfalls, adopt best practices, and successfully navigate the complexities of automation projects.

Key Insights

Best Practices

- **Effective Communication:**
    - **Essential for Alignment:** Clear and ongoing communication is identified as a crucial factor for the success of automation projects. Effective communication ensures all stakeholders are aligned with the project's objectives and progress.
    - **Goal Articulation and Updates:** It involves not just the initial articulation of goals but also providing regular updates throughout the project lifecycle to maintain transparency and engagement.
- **Iterative Development:**
    - **Flexibility in Implementation:** Adopting an iterative approach allows projects to be more flexible and responsive to feedback and changing requirements.
    - **Continuous Improvement:** This approach facilitates continuous improvement, where adjustments can be made in real-time, enhancing the project's outcome.

Challenges and Solutions

- **Integration Challenges:**
    - **Navigating Compatibility Issues:** One of the frequent challenges is integrating new automation technologies into existing systems. Compatibility issues can arise, leading to operational disruptions.
    - **Strategies for Integration:** Solutions include conducting thorough testing to identify and resolve issues and implementing the new technology in phases to ensure smooth integration.
- **Skill Gaps:**

- **Workforce Readiness:** Automation projects often highlight skill gaps in teams, particularly when new or advanced technologies are introduced.
- **Bridging the Gap:** Addressing this challenge typically involves targeted training programs tailored to the specific needs of the project. In some cases, bringing in external expertise can provide the necessary skill boost.

The insights from these lessons learned are invaluable for guiding future automation projects. By understanding and implementing effective communication strategies, embracing iterative development, navigating integration challenges thoughtfully, and addressing skill gaps proactively, organizations can enhance the success rate and impact of their mainframe automation initiatives.

Risk Management and Planning

Strategic Planning

- **Clear Roadmap:**
  - **Foundational Planning:** Establishing a clear strategic roadmap is vital. It sets the foundation for the project, outlining realistic goals, timelines, and measurable milestones.
  - **Guiding the Project:** This roadmap acts as a guide throughout the project lifecycle, ensuring that all efforts are aligned with the defined objectives and timelines.
- **Resource Allocation:**
  - **Balancing Resources:** Effective allocation of both human and technological resources is critical. It involves ensuring that the right mix of skills and technologies is available and optimally utilized throughout the project.
  - **Preventing Resource Shortfalls:** Proper planning in resource allocation helps prevent bottlenecks and shortfalls that could derail the project.

Mitigating Risks

- **Risk Identification:**
  - **Proactive Approach:** Early identification of potential risks is a key step in risk management. This includes foreseeing technical issues like compatibility problems and operational risks such as disruptions to business processes.
  - **Risk Assessment:** Regular risk assessments throughout the project help in staying aware of and prepared for potential challenges.
- **Contingency Planning:**
  - **Fallback Strategies:** Successful automation projects often have robust contingency plans in place. These plans outline

fallback options and strategies to address challenges that might arise unexpectedly.
    - **Adaptability:** Contingency planning ensures that the project can adapt and continue moving forward, even when faced with unforeseen obstacles or changes in the project environment.

The lessons learned in risk management and strategic planning are crucial for the success of mainframe automation projects. A well-defined strategic roadmap, effective resource allocation, proactive risk identification, and robust contingency planning are key components that guide a project to successful completion while navigating the complexities and uncertainties inherent in automation initiatives.

10.3. Innovations in Different Industries

Mainframe automation has significantly impacted various sectors, introducing innovations that have transformed traditional operations and processes. This section explores sector-specific innovations and emerging trends in different industries.

Sector-Specific Innovations

Finance and Banking

- **Automated Transaction Processing:**
  - **Efficiency in Operations:** Financial institutions have leveraged mainframe automation to enhance the speed and accuracy of transaction processing, leading to improved operational efficiency.
  - **Customer Satisfaction:** This automation has also contributed to better customer experience through faster transaction handling and reduced wait times.
- **Fraud Detection Systems:**
  - **Advanced Security Measures:** Mainframe automation has enabled the development of sophisticated fraud detection systems, using complex algorithms to identify and prevent fraudulent activities.
  - **Proactive Risk Management:** These systems have

significantly improved the sector's ability to manage risks and protect customer information.

Healthcare

- **Patient Data Management:**
    - **Streamlined Data Handling:** Automation in healthcare mainframes has revolutionized patient data management, making it more efficient and secure.
    - **Enhanced Patient Care:** This has facilitated better access to patient records, contributing to improved patient care and treatment outcomes.
- **Research Data Analysis:**
    - **Supporting Medical Research:** Mainframe automation has been instrumental in processing and analyzing large volumes of research data, accelerating medical research and discoveries.
    - **Data-Driven Insights:** The ability to handle complex data sets has led to more informed research findings and medical advancements.

Emerging Trends

Retail and E-commerce

- **Handling Transaction Volumes:**
    - **Scalability:** Retail and e-commerce sectors use mainframe automation to handle vast transaction volumes, especially during peak shopping periods.
    - **Customer Experience:** This automation ensures a seamless shopping experience for customers, even under high demand.
- **Customer Data Management:**
    - **Personalized Marketing:** Automated systems in

mainframes help manage and analyze customer data, leading to personalized marketing strategies and improved customer engagement.

Government and Public Sector

- **Efficient Public Record Management:**
    - **Accessibility and Security:** Government agencies utilize mainframe automation for efficient management of public records, enhancing both accessibility and security.
    - **Streamlined Services:** This leads to more streamlined and efficient public services, improving citizen engagement and satisfaction.
- **Data Processing:**
    - **Operational Efficiency:** Automation in government mainframes significantly boosts operational efficiency in data processing, from tax processing to welfare distribution.
    - **Policy Decision Support:** The ability to quickly process and analyze data aids in informed policy making and implementation.

In conclusion, mainframe automation has brought about groundbreaking innovations and efficiencies across various sectors. From finance and healthcare to retail and government, the integration of advanced automation capabilities has not only streamlined operations but also opened new avenues for service delivery and operational excellence.

Sector-Specific Innovations

The implementation of mainframe automation has brought about significant innovations in various sectors, notably in finance and banking as well as healthcare. These innovations have not only enhanced operational efficiencies but also transformed how services are delivered and decisions are made.

Finance and Banking

Automated Transaction Processing

- **Efficiency in Operations:**
    - Financial institutions are utilizing mainframe automation to accelerate the processing of transactions, enhancing both the speed and accuracy of these operations.
    - This efficiency has resulted in reduced processing times for customer transactions, contributing to more streamlined banking operations.
- **Customer Satisfaction:**
    - The quicker transaction handling and decreased wait times, courtesy of mainframe automation, have significantly enhanced the customer experience in the banking sector.

Fraud Detection Systems

- **Advanced Security Measures:**
    - Mainframe automation has facilitated the development of sophisticated fraud detection systems. These systems employ complex algorithms to effectively identify potential fraudulent activities.
    - The use of these advanced systems has bolstered the security measures in place within financial

institutions.

- **Proactive Risk Management:**
    - The automated fraud detection systems have played a critical role in improving the sector's ability to proactively manage risks and safeguard customer information, thereby enhancing trust and security in financial transactions.

Healthcare

Patient Data Management

- **Streamlined Data Handling:**
    - Automation in healthcare mainframes has revolutionized the way patient data is managed, leading to more efficient and secure data handling processes.
    - This has resulted in streamlined access to patient records, facilitating quicker and more accurate diagnoses and treatments.
- **Enhanced Patient Care:**
    - Improved access to patient records, thanks to mainframe automation, has been instrumental in enhancing the quality of patient care and treatment outcomes.

Research Data Analysis

- **Supporting Medical Research:**
    - Mainframe automation has been crucial in processing and analyzing extensive volumes of research data, thereby accelerating medical research and leading to faster discoveries.
    - This has been particularly beneficial in complex

medical research areas where large datasets are common.

- **Data-Driven Insights:**
    - The capability to handle and analyze complex data sets efficiently has led to more informed research findings, facilitating medical advancements and contributing to the body of medical knowledge.

In conclusion, the innovations brought by mainframe automation in finance and banking, and healthcare have led to significant improvements not only in operational efficiencies but also in customer experience and patient care. These advancements highlight the transformative impact of automation across different sectors, paving the way for future innovations and improvements.

Emerging Trends

The adoption of mainframe automation in various sectors is not only enhancing operational efficiencies but also revolutionizing customer experiences and public services. These emerging trends in the retail, e-commerce, government, and public sector highlight the expansive impact of mainframe automation.

Retail and E-commerce

Handling Transaction Volumes

- **Scalability:**
    - Retail and e-commerce businesses leverage mainframe automation to efficiently handle large transaction volumes, a crucial aspect during peak shopping periods like sales and holidays.
    - This scalability ensures that these sectors can cope with sudden surges in demand without compromising on transaction processing times or system stability.

Customer Experience

- **Seamless Shopping Experience:**
    - Automation contributes significantly to providing a seamless shopping experience for customers, even during periods of high demand, by ensuring quick and efficient transaction processing.
    - The ability to handle high transaction volumes smoothly plays a key role in maintaining customer satisfaction and loyalty.

Customer Data Management

- **Personalized Marketing:**
    - Mainframe automation aids in the effective

management and analysis of customer data, which is crucial for developing personalized marketing strategies.
    - This targeted approach leads to improved customer engagement and can significantly enhance the effectiveness of marketing campaigns.

Government and Public Sector

Efficient Public Record Management

- **Accessibility and Security:**
    - Government agencies are employing mainframe automation for the efficient and secure management of public records. This not only enhances accessibility but also ensures the security of sensitive information.
    - Automation in record management facilitates easier access for citizens and officials, while maintaining strict data security protocols.

Streamlined Services

- **Improving Public Service Delivery:**
    - The automation of record management systems leads to more streamlined and efficient public services, improving citizen engagement and overall satisfaction with public services.

Data Processing

- **Operational Efficiency:**
    - In government mainframes, automation significantly boosts operational efficiency in various data processing tasks, such as tax

processing, welfare distribution, and public record maintenance.
    - This efficiency is essential for the timely and accurate delivery of public services.
- **Policy Decision Support:**
    - The ability to quickly process and analyze large volumes of data supports informed policymaking and implementation, enabling government agencies to make data-driven decisions that better serve the public interest.

These emerging trends in mainframe automation across retail, e-commerce, and government sectors demonstrate the versatile applications and benefits of automation. From enhancing customer experiences and personalizing marketing strategies to streamlining public services and supporting policy decisions, mainframe automation is proving to be a pivotal technology in modernizing and improving various industry operations.

Chapter 11. Conclusion

11.1. Recap of Key Learnings

Throughout this exploration of mainframe automation, several key learnings have emerged:

- **Evolution and Relevance:** The evolution of mainframes has shown their lasting relevance in the modern technological landscape. Despite advancements in other areas of computing, mainframes remain pivotal due to their reliability, security, and processing power.
- **Integration of New Technologies:** The integration of AI, machine learning, and cloud computing into mainframe systems has been a significant step forward, enhancing capabilities in data processing, predictive analytics, and system management.
- **Sector-Specific Innovations:** Different sectors have uniquely leveraged mainframe automation to revolutionize their operations, from finance and healthcare to retail and government, showcasing the versatility of mainframe applications.
- **Best Practices and Challenges:** Lessons from various case studies emphasize the importance of effective communication, iterative development, strategic planning,

and risk management in successful mainframe automation projects.

11.2. The Future of Mainframe in the Automated World

Looking ahead, the future of mainframe computing in an automated world appears robust:

- **Continued Innovation:** Mainframes are expected to continue evolving, integrating further with cutting-edge technologies like blockchain and quantum computing.
- **Adaptation to New Challenges:** As cybersecurity threats and data demands grow, mainframes are poised to meet these challenges with enhanced security measures and processing capabilities.
- **Strategic Role in IT Infrastructure:** Mainframes will likely maintain a strategic role in IT infrastructures, especially in handling critical, high-volume transactions and data-intensive tasks.

11.3. Final Thoughts and Advice for Practitioners

For practitioners in the field of mainframe automation:

- **Embrace Continuous Learning:** Stay abreast of the latest technological advancements and industry trends. Continuous learning is key to adapting to the evolving landscape.
- **Focus on Integration and Adaptability:** Prioritize the integration of new technologies into existing systems and strive for adaptability in your approaches to mainframe automation.
- **Collaborate and Innovate:** Foster collaborations with technology partners and encourage innovation within your

teams. This collaboration is crucial for driving forward the capabilities of mainframe systems.

- **Prioritize Strategic Planning:** Engage in thorough strategic planning and risk management to navigate the complexities of mainframe automation projects successfully.

In conclusion, mainframe automation stands at a fascinating juncture, balancing its rich legacy with the prospects of future innovations. For practitioners, the journey involves continuous learning, strategic adaptation, and an openness to innovation, ensuring that mainframes remain a vital and dynamic component of the global IT infrastructure.

11.1. Recap of Key Learnings

The journey through the landscape of mainframe automation has revealed several critical insights and developments that underscore the enduring significance and evolving nature of mainframe technology.

- **Evolution and Relevance:** Mainframes have demonstrated remarkable resilience and adaptability. Despite the rapid evolution of technology, they continue to be a cornerstone in critical computing environments due to their unparalleled reliability, robust security, and exceptional processing power.
- **Integration of New Technologies:** The incorporation of advanced technologies like AI, machine learning, and cloud computing into mainframes marks a significant evolution. This integration has expanded the capabilities of mainframes beyond traditional boundaries, enabling enhanced data processing, sophisticated predictive analytics, and more efficient system management.
- **Sector-Specific Innovations:** The application of mainframe automation across various sectors illustrates its wide-reaching impact. From transforming financial

transactions and healthcare data management to revolutionizing retail operations and public sector services, mainframes have proven their versatility and adaptability in addressing diverse industry needs.

- **Best Practices and Challenges:** Insights from case studies highlight crucial factors for successful mainframe automation projects. Effective communication, an iterative approach to development, strategic planning, and comprehensive risk management have emerged as best practices. These elements are vital in navigating the complexities and maximizing the benefits of mainframe automation.

These key learnings reflect the dynamic interplay between technological innovation and practical application in the realm of mainframe automation. They emphasize the necessity of continuous adaptation and strategic foresight in leveraging the full potential of mainframes in today's rapidly evolving digital landscape.

11.2. The Future of Mainframe in the Automated World

As we look towards the future, mainframe computing in the context of automation and technological evolution presents a landscape of both challenges and opportunities. The role of mainframes is not diminishing; rather, it is becoming more integral and adaptive to new technological paradigms.

- **Continued Innovation:**
    - **Integration with Advanced Technologies:** The journey of mainframes is marked by continuous innovation. The integration with technologies like blockchain for enhanced security and quantum computing for unprecedented processing capabilities is on the horizon. These integrations will open up new possibilities for mainframe applications, making them more powerful and versatile.
    - **Expanding Capabilities:** As mainframes evolve, they will likely become more adept at handling complex, data-intensive tasks that are beyond the scope of current technologies, further solidifying their position in the computing world.
- **Adaptation to New Challenges:**
    - **Cybersecurity:** In an era of increasing digital threats,

mainframes are expected to evolve to meet these challenges head-on. With enhanced security measures, mainframes will continue to be trusted with sensitive and critical data, maintaining their reputation for being highly secure platforms.

    - **Meeting Growing Data Demands:** As data becomes increasingly central to business operations, mainframes are expected to adapt to handle growing data demands efficiently, leveraging their inherent strengths in processing and managing large volumes of data.

- **Strategic Role in IT Infrastructure:**
    - **Handling Critical Operations:** Mainframes are projected to maintain a strategic role in IT infrastructures, particularly in sectors where handling high-volume transactions and managing large datasets are crucial. This includes finance, healthcare, government, and more.
    - **Foundation of Hybrid Systems:** In the emerging hybrid IT landscapes, combining cloud and traditional infrastructures, mainframes will likely serve as the backbone for critical operations, ensuring stability and reliability.

In conclusion, the future of mainframe computing in an automated and technologically advanced world is bright and promising. With their continued innovation, adaptation to new challenges, and strategic role in IT infrastructure, mainframes are poised to remain at the forefront of enterprise computing, underpinning the digital operations of numerous industries.

11.3. Final Thoughts and Advice for Practitioners

As we conclude our exploration of mainframe automation, it's important to offer guidance to those in the field who are navigating this evolving landscape. For practitioners, from engineers to IT managers, embracing a forward-thinking and proactive approach is key to success in this domain.

- **Embrace Continuous Learning:**
    - **Stay Informed:** The technology sector, especially mainframe computing, is in a constant state of evolution. Staying informed about the latest advancements, whether in AI, blockchain, or quantum computing, is crucial.
    - **Lifelong Learning:** Adopting a mindset of continuous learning and professional development will enable practitioners to remain competent and competitive in their field.
- **Focus on Integration and Adaptability:**
    - **Seamless Integration:** As new technologies emerge, the ability to integrate them seamlessly into existing mainframe systems becomes vital. This requires a deep understanding of both legacy systems and new technologies.
    - **Adaptive Strategies:** Developing adaptive strategies that

can quickly respond to changes in technology and business needs is essential for ensuring that mainframe systems remain relevant and efficient.

- **Collaborate and Innovate:**
    - **Partnership and Teamwork:** Building strong collaborations with technology partners, vendors, and within teams can lead to innovative solutions and advancements in mainframe automation.
    - **Cultivate Innovation:** Encourage a culture of innovation where new ideas and approaches are welcomed and explored. This can lead to groundbreaking developments and solutions.
- **Prioritize Strategic Planning:**
    - **Comprehensive Planning:** Engage in thorough and strategic planning for all mainframe automation projects. This includes understanding project objectives, defining clear goals, and mapping out detailed execution plans.
    - **Risk Management:** Effective risk management is crucial. Anticipate potential challenges and develop contingency plans to mitigate risks, ensuring the smooth progression and success of mainframe automation projects.

In summary, the field of mainframe automation offers a dynamic and challenging environment. For practitioners, success hinges on their ability to continually learn, adapt, innovate, and strategically plan. By embracing these principles, they can not only navigate the complexities of today's technological landscape but also shape the future of mainframe computing.

Appendix A. Glossary of Terms

In the realm of mainframe automation, numerous technical terms and concepts are frequently used. This glossary provides definitions for some of the key terms to aid in understanding and navigating the subject matter.

1. **Mainframe:** A powerful computer used primarily by large organizations for critical applications, bulk data processing, and large-scale transaction processing.
2. **Automation:** The use of technology to perform tasks with minimal human intervention. In mainframe contexts, it often refers to the use of software to manage and control the operations of the mainframe.
3. **AI (Artificial Intelligence):** A branch of computer science dealing with the simulation of intelligent behavior in computers, enabling them to perform tasks that typically require human intelligence.
4. **Machine Learning:** A subset of AI that involves the development of algorithms that can learn and make predictions or decisions based on data.
5. **Cloud Computing:** The delivery of different services through the internet, including data storage, servers, databases, networking, and software.

6. **Blockchain:** A system of recording information in a way that makes it difficult or impossible to change, hack, or cheat the system, often used for secure transactions and data storage.
7. **Quantum Computing:** A type of computing that uses quantum-mechanical phenomena, such as superposition and entanglement, to perform operations on data.
8. **Cybersecurity:** The practice of protecting systems, networks, and programs from digital attacks.
9. **Predictive Analytics:** The use of data, statistical algorithms, and machine learning techniques to identify the likelihood of future outcomes based on historical data.
10. **Scalability:** The capability of a system to handle a growing amount of work, or its potential to be enlarged to accommodate that growth.
11. **Fraud Detection Systems:** Software systems that help in identifying attempts at fraud, often used in banking and financial transactions.
12. **Data Analytics:** The science of analyzing raw data to make conclusions about that information, often using specialized systems and software.
13. **Risk Management:** The process of identifying, assessing, and controlling threats to an organization's capital and earnings.
14. **IT Infrastructure:** The combination of hardware, software, network resources, and services required for the existence, operation, and management of an enterprise IT environment.

This glossary is not exhaustive but covers some of the fundamental concepts and terms relevant to the field of mainframe automation.

Appendix B. Resources for Further Learning

To delve deeper into the world of mainframe automation and stay abreast of the latest trends and developments, a variety of resources are available. These resources range from online courses and professional certifications to publications and forums. Below is a list of recommended resources for further learning and exploration.

1. **Online Courses and Certifications:**
    - **Coursera, Udemy, and edX:** Offer various courses on topics like AI, machine learning, cloud computing, and cybersecurity which are relevant to mainframe automation.
    - **IBM Learning:** Provides specific courses and certifications for mainframe technologies.
2. **Books and Publications:**
    - **"Mainframe Basics for Security Professionals: Getting Started with RACF" by Ori Pomerantz et al.:** Offers insights into mainframe security.
    - **"IBM Z Connectivity Handbook" by Bill White and IBM Redbooks:** A guide to understanding mainframe connectivity options.
3. **Professional Organizations and Forums:**

- **SHARE.org:** A volunteer-run user group for IBM mainframe users, offering conferences, webinars, and networking opportunities.
- **Mainframe DevOps Community:** A community for those interested in the modern development practices that are being adopted on the mainframe.

4. **Technical Journals and Websites:**
    - **IBM Systems Magazine:** Provides articles, whitepapers, and case studies on mainframe technology.
    - **The Enterprisers Project:** Offers a collection of articles and resources on the role of IT and mainframe in the enterprise world.
5. **Podcasts and Webinars:**
    - **Terminal Talk:** A podcast about mainframes and mainframe-related topics.
    - **IBM Webinars:** Regular webinars on various mainframe topics, including automation and new technology integrations.
6. **Industry Conferences and Workshops:**
    - **IBM Think:** An annual conference that covers various aspects of IBM technology, including mainframes.
    - **Tech Conferences by Gartner and Forrester:** Often feature sessions and workshops on mainframes and enterprise computing.
7. **Social Media Groups:**
    - **LinkedIn Groups:** Such as "Mainframe Professionals" or "Mainframe Experts" where professionals share insights and news.

- **Twitter:** Following hashtags like #mainframe or industry leaders can provide real-time updates and discussions.

8. **Vendor-Specific Training:**
    - **IBM Mainframe Training Programs:** IBM offers extensive training materials and courses specific to its mainframe products.

These resources provide a wealth of information and learning opportunities for anyone interested in mainframe automation, from beginners to experienced professionals. Engaging with these resources can enhance knowledge, spark innovation, and provide networking opportunities with other professionals in the field.

Epilogue

As we close the book on "Next-Gen Mainframe: Mastering Modern Automation Techniques", we reflect on the journey through the intricate world of mainframe automation. This exploration has not only highlighted the enduring significance of mainframes in the modern technological era but also underscored their evolving role amidst rapid technological advancements.

The Journey Recapitulated:

We delved into the history and evolution of mainframes, understanding their foundational role in computing history and their adaptation to contemporary demands. The exploration of modern automation tools and technologies revealed how mainframes are being reinvented, integrating with AI, machine learning, and cloud computing to meet the challenges of big data, cybersecurity, and the need for more efficient processing.

Industry-Specific Impacts:

The impact of mainframe automation across various sectors – from finance and healthcare to retail and government – demonstrated its versatile application in addressing diverse industry needs. These insights illustrated how mainframe automation is not just a matter of technological advancement but also a driver of operational efficiency and innovation.

Preparing for the Future:

Looking ahead, the journey into the future of mainframes in an automated world showed us a landscape where continuous innovation, adaptability, and strategic integration are key. For practitioners, the path forward is paved with continuous learning, embracing change, and fostering collaborations.

Final Reflections:

Mainframe automation stands as a testament to the incredible journey of technological evolution. It's a field that combines the robust legacy of traditional computing with the dynamic possibilities of the future. As this book concludes, it leaves us with a sense of both accomplishment in what has been achieved and anticipation for what is yet to come in the ever-evolving story of mainframe computing.

In this narrative of progress and adaptation, "Next-Gen Mainframe: Mastering Modern Automation Techniques" serves not just as a repository of knowledge but also as a beacon, guiding enthusiasts and professionals alike towards the future of technology. As mainframes continue to evolve and adapt, they remain an integral part of the technological landscape, echoing the timeless dance of progress and perseverance.

Don't miss out!

Visit the website below and you can sign up to receive emails whenever Isaac Nangan publishes a new book. There's no charge and no obligation.

https://books2read.com/r/B-A-SPRBB-BOVUC

BOOKS 2 READ

Connecting independent readers to independent writers.

Did you love *Next-Gen Mainframe: Mastering Modern Automation Techniques*? Then you should read *Modern Mainframe Mastery: Navigating the New Era of Systems Management*[1] by Isaac Nangan!

2

In the ever-evolving landscape of information technology, mainframe systems have stood the test of time, consistently proving their worth in the world's most demanding computing environments. Despite their longevity, the perception of mainframes as relics of a bygone era is a misconception. Today's mainframe systems are at the forefront of modern computing, driving innovation and supporting critical operations in numerous industries.

"Modern Mainframe Mastery: Navigating the New Era of System Management" is conceived as a comprehensive guide for IT

1. https://books2read.com/u/mZYwOJ

2. https://books2read.com/u/mZYwOJ

professionals, students, and enthusiasts who aim to understand the fusion of traditional mainframe technology with contemporary methodologies. This book is not just a technical manual but a journey through the evolution and resurgence of mainframe systems in the context of modern IT practices.

The goal of this book is twofold. Firstly, to demystify the notion that mainframes are an outdated technology, and secondly, to provide a clear understanding of how modern methodologies like Agile, DevOps, cloud computing, and AI can be harmoniously integrated with mainframe systems management. It is intended for those who are just beginning their journey in the realm of mainframes, as well as seasoned professionals seeking to update their skills with the latest trends and practices.

Throughout the book, you will find a blend of theoretical concepts, practical applications, real-world case studies, and expert insights. Each chapter is crafted to build upon the previous ones, gradually elevating the reader's understanding from the basic architecture of mainframes to the complexities of managing these systems using modern techniques.

The mainframe is not just a piece of technology; it is a testament to the enduring ingenuity of the human mind in the field of computing. As we look towards the future, the mainframe continues to adapt, evolve, and integrate with emerging technologies, ensuring its relevance and critical role in the IT infrastructure for years to come.

Also by Isaac Nangan

Mainframes

Mastering z/OS Management Facility: A Comprehensive Guide to Mainframe Innovation

How to Harness the Power of Jenkins on Mainframes: A Comprehensive Guide

Mainframe Revolution: Harnessing AI for Next-Gen Computing

Encapsulating Legacy: A Guide to Service-Oriented Architecture in Mainframe Systems

Mainframe Revival: Embracing Containerization

Modern Mainframe Mastery: Navigating the New Era of Systems Management

Next-Gen Mainframe: Mastering Modern Automation Techniques

www.ingramcontent.com/pod-product-compliance
Lightning Source LLC
LaVergne TN
LVHW050302210926
848481LV00014BA/369
* 9 7 8 9 8 1 5 1 9 4 4 3 2 *